Includes Texas Hold'em

PLAY POKER LIKE A PRO

The Rules of the Game

Wesley R. Young

Publications International, Ltd.

Wesley R. Young is a poker player, freelance writer, and college professor. He has a master's degree in business administration and a bachelor's degree in mathematics. His poker experience includes more than 15 years of play. Young maintains a poker Web site at www.pokermonger.com.

Louis Weber, CEO
Publications International, Ltd.
7373 North Cicero Avenue
Lincolnwood, Illinois 60712

Manufactured in China.

8 7 6 5 4 3 2 1

ISBN: 1-4127-1154-1

CONTENTS

IMPROVE YOUR POKER SKILLS

Right now is the best time to be a poker player. In fact, new players are entering into the game every day in large numbers. As more people seek opportunities to play poker, more poker rooms and Web sites are opening up. As a result, the coverage of poker on television and the number of books and amount of information made available increases, which in turn bring more players into the game. This cycle continues to feed itself so that the popularity of poker is now at an all-time high.

This upsurging interest in poker, particularly Texas Hold'em, is great whether you have been playing poker for years or are just starting. Experienced players never have to worry about finding a good Hold'em game at any time of the day or night. Beginning players can start playing without risking any money or play for limits as low as pennies. Because of the ability to play more than one game at a time and the speed of the game on the Internet (there's no downtime waiting for a game or shuffling), people are playing thousands of hands a week. Younger players are gaining the experience in a few years that used to take decades of learning.

We all want to win when we play poker. No person enters a game seeking anything less, and that's why *Play Poker Like a Pro* is the perfect fit for you. If you are a beginning player, this book will jump-start your learning process. Or, if you are an experienced player, it has numerous insights, especially into Texas Hold'em, that will give you an edge against other experienced Hold'em players.

This book starts with the basics, such as how to play, and then advances through basic strategy into advanced strategy. No matter what your experience or skill level, you will improve your game by reading and using the strategies contained here. You'll also find questions to test your newfound knowledge at the end of some of the chapters along with the answers at the back of the book. So increase your poker skills, and good luck at the tables.

Chapter One
GET ACQUAINTED

Did you ever wonder where poker originated? For a quick lesson on poker history and the basics of poker, read on!

Many people were introduced to poker by seeing it played in the saloons in Western movies, and the poker game played was most often 5-Card Draw. Some people may also have heard stories of riverboat gamblers on the Mississippi River. For these reasons, a lot of people grew up believing poker began in America in the 1900s, and the only poker game ever played was 5-Card Draw. Actually, both assumptions are false. The origin of poker and playing cards is briefly discussed in this chapter. In the next chapter, considerable time will be spent discussing the hottest poker game in any town—Texas Hold'em.

Migration and Evolution

The actual origin of poker is not known. Some say the Chinese played with cards as early as the tenth century A.D. In another part of the world, archaeologists recovered fragments of cardlike items dating to the twelfth or thirteenth century in Egypt. Of course, we don't know what the Egyptians used these cards for, but it could have been the first form of poker. We do know that in the sixteenth century people in India played a betting game called *Ganjifa*, which used a deck of 96 cards; and in the seventeenth century the Persians played a five-player card game, which they called *As Nas*, using 25 cards in five suits.

The current 52-card deck is often credited to European countries. In the fifteenth century, France introduced the current suits of clubs, diamonds, hearts, and spades in a game called *Poque*. It is quite possible that the word "poker" is derived from that word. Others, however, claim that the word "poker" comes from the German card game *pochspiel* or the German bluffing game *pochen*, which dates back to the sixteenth century. Also, the British are credited with the introduction of games called "Brag" and "Faro," which were played in many saloons in the Old West.

Eventually, poker migrated to the United States in the late eighteenth century and continued to spread throughout North America. Variations of poque called "draw" and "stud" became popular during the Civil War. These terms are still used today.

A Couple of Things You Should Know

A basic explanation of key poker terms follows. If you have experience playing poker, you can skim this material. On the other hand, if you have never played poker, this is a good place to start.

Ranking of Hands

In order to succeed at poker you must memorize the ranking of hands. All poker players

should know, for instance, that a flush beats a straight. Here is the ranking from the strongest to the weakest hand.

- **Royal Flush**—A royal flush is a straight flush with the ace as the highest of five cards. For example: ♠A-♠K-♠Q-♠J-♠T.
- **Straight Flush**—A straight flush is a straight all of the same suit. For example: ♥9-♥8-♥7-♥6-♥5. In the case of two straight flushes during one hand, the one containing the highest card is the winner. The pot is split if both players have the same high card. (A "hand" can mean either the cards in a player's hand or a round of play; in this case, "hand" refers to a round of play.)
- **Four of a Kind**—Four cards of the same rank. For example: ♥9-♣9-♦9-♠9. Four of a kind is often referred to as "quads." The highest four of a kind is four aces followed by four kings on down to four twos.
- **Full House**—A full house consists of three of a kind and two of a kind. For example: ♦K-♠K-♥K-♠6-♣6. This would be called "kings full of sixes." If there are two full houses during one hand, the one with the largest three of a kind wins. In Texas Hold'em, it is possible for two players to have the same three of a kind; in those situations the pairs determine the winner. If two players have identical hands, the pot is split.

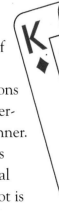

Kings full of sixes

- **Flush**—A flush consists of five cards of the same suit. For example: ♦K-♦J-♦9-♦7-♦2. In the event of two flushes during one hand, the flush with the highest card wins. If they are the same rank, it goes to the next highest card, and on down to the fifth card if necessary. If the two hands are identical, the pot is split between the winners.
- **Straight**—A straight consists of five cards of any suit in order. For example: ♦Q-♠J-♣T-♣9-♥8. As with the other hands, in the event of two straights, the one that starts with the highest rank wins. Aces can be used as a high card above a king or as a low card below a two to make a straight. You can't, however, use a king, ace, two sequence; and an ace below a two cannot be used as the high card.
- **Three of a kind**—Three of the same rank. For example: ♠Q-♦Q-♥Q. Three of a kind is often called a "set" or "trips."
- **Two Pairs**—Four cards of two ranks. For example: ♣J-♦J-♥6-♣6. This would be called "Jacks up." In the event of two players holding two pairs at the same time, the highest pair wins. If both high pairs are the same rank, then the higher second pair wins. If both high and low pairs are the same, the pot is split.
- **One Pair**—Two cards of the same rank. For example: ♣8-♥8. If two players have an identical pair, such as two aces, the next highest card in each player's hand is compared to see who wins. This is often called a "kicker" and is frequently necessary in Texas Hold'em. (The kicker will be explained in more detail in the next chapter.)

CARD ABBREVIATIONS

Abbreviations for cards and their ranks will often appear. Refer to this list of abbreviations.

A	Ace (also known as a "bullet")
K	King (also known as a "cowboy")
Q	Queen
J	Jack (also known as a "hook")
T	Ten
9	Nine
8	Eight
7	Seven
6	Six
5	Five
4	Four
3	Three
2	Two (also known as a "deuce" or a "duck")
AA	Pair of aces
AK	Ace and king (this pair is known as "big slick")
Q9s	Queen and nine, suited (of the same suit). (The s means suited, so if it were Q9 without the s, that indicates the cards are of different suits.)

- **High Card**—In the event no player has a hand containing at least one pair, the hand with the highest card is the winner. The rank of cards starting from highest is ace, king, queen, jack, 10, 9, 8, 7, 6, 5, 4, 3, 2, and 1 if the ace is used as a 1.

Blinds

Most Hold'em (short for Texas Hold'em) poker games require players to post blinds (initial bets) before any cards are dealt in order to stimulate action. Usually there are two blinds—a small blind and a big blind—in each playing round. The blinds rotate one place to the left each hand. The small blind is to the left of the dealer and acts first in all betting rounds except the first and is usually half the amount of the big blind. The big blind is to the left of the small blind and is usually equal to the minimum bet at whatever limit that is being played. On the first round of betting, the big blind acts last since that player already has a full bet in the pot.

If you are entering an existing Hold'em game, you will probably be required to post the big blind in order to play. If your seat is near the big blind on your right, you will probably want to wait until the big blind is at your position. If you are already in a Hold'em game and you leave the table and miss the blinds, you will be required to post both blinds in order to resume play, or you can wait until the big blind comes to your position.

In Draw, Stud, and other poker games, antes are required of each player. The ante varies according to the agreement of the players or according to the rules of a casino or poker room. In some cases, such as in a tournament, both antes and blinds may be required.

Chapter Two

NOT JUST FOR TEXANS

Whether you are a beginner or an experienced player, by the time you finish this chapter, you should be playing like a pro.

Texas Hold'em is currently the most popular form of poker by far. It is a game that has all the elements that make poker such a wonderful pastime. There are opportunities to bluff, gamble, apply mathematical skills, get lucky or unlucky, use strategy, and possibly win large sums of money. Hold'em is offered in virtually every card room and is on many Internet sites. Meanwhile, an increasing number of poker players play Texas Hold'em at home. In this chapter you will learn how to play, the differences among the various limit games (limit, no limit, and pot limit), and basic and advanced strategies. If you are new to poker, study the previous chapter on the basics of poker and the first part of this chapter in order to get a firm grasp of the basics of Texas Hold'em before jumping into the strategy sections.

How to Play

Texas Hold'em is usually played with nine or ten players at a full table with a rotating blind system as discussed in the "Blinds" section on pages 14–15. In tournament play, an ante is also sometimes used in addition to the rotating blind. After the blinds and antes (if applicable) are placed, each player is dealt two down cards (called hole cards). Then each player starting with the player to the left of the big blind has an opportunity to call the big blind, raise the bet, or fold. When the action gets to the player in the small blind position, he/she can call the partial bet, raise the bet, or fold. The player in the big blind has the option to raise or check if there are no raises as he/she already has a full bet in the pot. Any player who calls the big blind and has the pot raised behind him/her then has the option to call the raise or reraise the pot.

Most limit Hold'em games have a three bet limit per round, which means there can be only three raises per round of betting. In this case, "round" refers to a series of checks, bets, calls, raises, and folds during a single session of betting or nonbetting. After the first round of betting, three community cards (called the flop) are placed face up in the center of the table. A second round of betting is now conducted starting with the player to the left of the button (dealer). Each player still active in the hand may check or bet. After a bet, each player may call the bet, raise, reraise if there was a raise, or fold.

The fourth community card (called the turn or fourth street) is then placed face up in the center of the table followed by another round of betting. In most limit games, the amount of a bet on the turn and river (last community card) is double the amount in the first two rounds.

Finally, the last community card (called the river or fifth street) is placed face up in the center of the table, and the last round of betting is conducted. After all bets have been placed, a showdown occurs, which simply means that players still in the hand show their hole cards to see who wins the pot.

Players use any combination of their hole cards and the community cards to form the best five-card hand possible. Players can use both of their hole cards and three community cards, one hole card and four community cards, or all five community cards. Players who use the five community cards to form their best hand can usually win only part of the pot or lose as everyone can use all five community cards. An example would be when the board shows ♠A-♠K-♠Q-♠J-♠T, then everyone left in the hand will split the pot as the board shows a royal flush, which is the best hand possible.

Royal flush

Playing Limit Hold'em

Limit Hold'em is played with a fixed blind structure and fixed betting limits on each round. The big blind is usually equal to the smallest size bet, and the small blind is half the big blind. The first two rounds of betting use the small bet, and the last two use the large bet. For example: In a 2/4 (2 dollar/4 dollar) limit game, the small blind is $1, the big blind is $2, the first two rounds of betting are in $2 increments, and the last two rounds are in $4 increments.

A few card rooms offer spread limit Hold'em. Spread limit Hold'em is stated as 2/10 or something similar. The blinds are the same as fixed limit: For example, in the 2/10 games, the small blind is $1, and the big blind is $2. The difference is that all other bets in spread limit may be anywhere from $2 to $10. The only additional rule is if a player reraises another player, the raise must be at least the size of the previous raise. In brick-and-mortar card rooms, the smallest limit available is usually 1/2 or 2/4 and the largest can be 10,000/20,000 or higher. Most recreational players play 1/2, 2/4, 3/6, 4/8, 5/10, or 10/20. As a general rule, the higher the limits, the better the competition.

For beginners, some Internet sites offer stakes as low as .01/.02, as well as the option to use play money and risk nothing at all. Some professional poker players play only limit Hold'em and make a very good living at it. Becoming a profitable limit Hold'em player is about starting hand selection, understanding pot odds, and discipline, as well as understanding betting patterns. Each of these elements of Texas Hold'em is discussed in detail later in this chapter.

Playing No-Limit or Pot-Limit Hold'em

If you watch poker on television, no-limit Texas Hold'em is probably the format you are

watching. It is most often used in tournament play, but it is also offered in many card rooms as a ring game (nontournament game). In no-limit, players still post blinds according to a set schedule depending on the house rules and often are required to place antes as well. What makes no-limit different from limit is that placed bets after the blinds can be for any amount up to the total amount a player has on the table.

In a no-limit tournament, making just one mistake can knock a player out of the game. No-limit also allows many opportunities for better players to bluff opponents out of a hand. Often a player who goes all-in (raises with all of his/her chips) is called by someone who doesn't have as many chips. In this case, if the player who started the hand with more chips loses the hand, he/she gets back any amount over what the other player had to start the hand. For example: Player 1 goes all-in with $200, and player 2 calls but has only $100. Player 1 loses but gets back $100, and they play out the next hand for the remaining $200 ($100 from player 1 and $100 from player 2) in the pot. (No-limit Hold'em is discussed in greater detail later in this chapter and in Chapter Nine "Tournament Play.")

The betting in pot-limit Texas Hold'em is not as structured as limit Hold'em but not as risky as no-limit Hold'em. The rules for blinds remain the same, but you can bet only up to the amount that is in the pot. So, for players who want more freedom in their betting than is allowed in limit Hold'em, but want to stay away from the kind of action involved in no-limit Hold'em, pot-limit Hold'em is the preferred game of choice.

Basic Strategy

In this section many of the basic strategies involved in becoming a winning Hold'em player are discussed. If you are a new player or a player with some experience looking to take your game to the next level, mastering the concepts in this section will start you on the right foot or greatly improve your game.

Position

The position at which a player starts a hand will have a great bearing on how the hand is played. The best position in Hold'em, whether limit, no-limit, or pot-limit, is the dealer position (often called the button). The player with the button is the last to act in each round except for the first round of betting (the big blind acts last in the first round). The reason this is such an advantage is that the button gets to see what everyone else does before he/she has to act. This leads to opportunities to steal a pot with a marginal hand and allows good players to win the maximum amount with their good hand. It also allows the good players to minimize their losses in certain situations.

The worst position is the player to the left of the big blind (often called under-the-gun). Your biggest decision in Hold'em is the first one you must make: whether to play a hand or not. On average, profitable players enter the pot with better hands than other players. Before you enter a pot, you want as much information as possible. When under-the-gun, you have no information about what any of the other players are going to do. This puts you at a distinct disadvantage. For these reasons, you can often play weaker hands the closer you

get to the button. Let's assume that the small blind is in seat 1, the big blind is in seat 2, and the button is in seat 10. The players in seats 3, 4, and 5 are in early position, seats 6 and 7 are in middle position, and seats 8, 9, and 10 are in late position. You will learn in the next section that some hands can be played in the middle or late positions that cannot be played in the early positions.

Let's think about that statement for a minute. Considering the fact that 10 percent of the time you will be in the big blind, which will often let you see the flop for free, if you are to be a winning player, you won't enter many other pots—only one to one and a half on average each round other than when you are the big blind.

Many players will call a half bet in the small blind with any two cards. After reading this

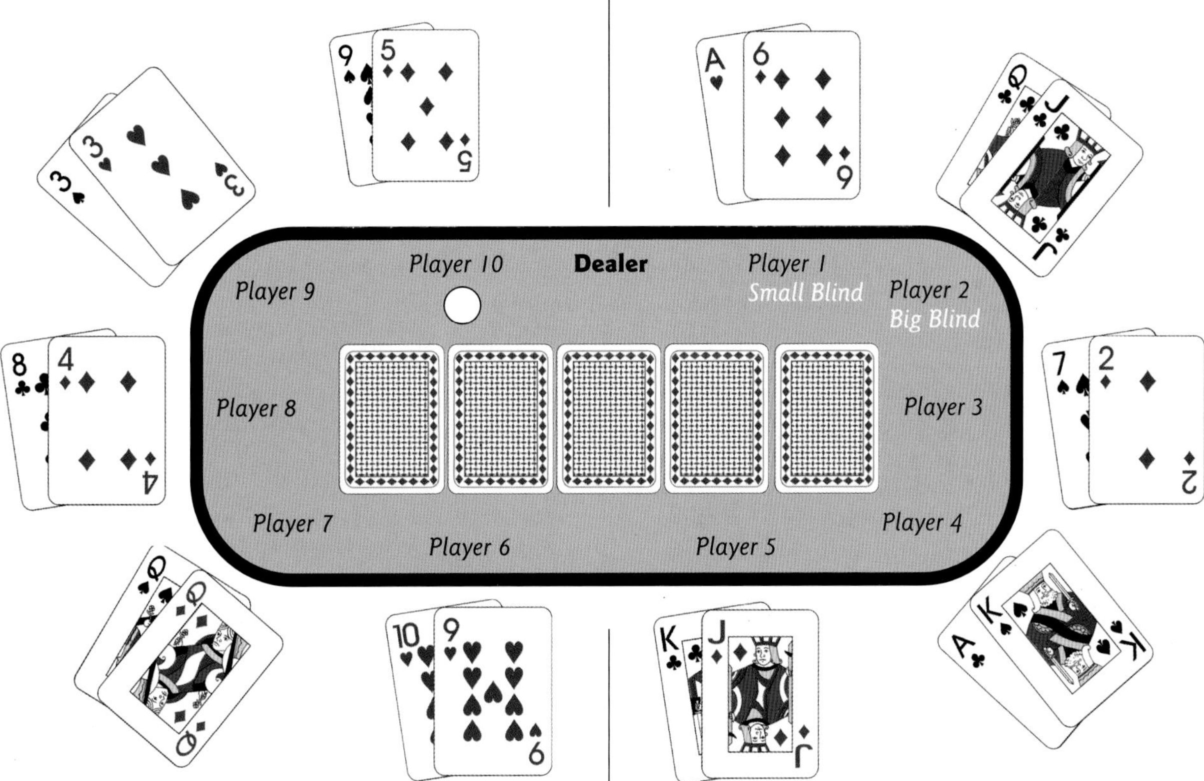

Starting Hand Selection

If your goal is to become a winning Texas Hold'em player, this section is invaluable. As stated above, the most important decision you make as a Hold'em player is whether or not to enter the pot (or play for the pot). Almost all losing Hold'em players play far too many hands. Winning Hold'em players see the flop only between 20 and 25 percent of the time.

book, hopefully you won't play this way as it can cost you considerable money in the long run. This one error, when done repeatedly, can be the difference between winning and losing.

Let's discuss what hands can be played from each position under a variety of circumstances. You should refer to this section often and eventually memorize it as you gain experience. As with everything in poker, rarely is any

decision set in stone. The following are solid guidelines to help you understand what to look for in each position. Many things will go into each decision you make, such as who enters the pot before you, if the pot has been raised, how loose or tight the other players are, and your table image. Each of these factors will be discussed later in the book. What is important to remember is that these guidelines are a good starting point, but through experience you will tweak them to best fit your playing style.

Many professional players play more hands than recommended, but their post-flop play and ability to read other players is superior to most people's abilities. This allows them to outplay their opponents and make up for the difference in starting hand composition after the flop.

These recommendations are also geared toward low-limit Texas Hold'em, such as 1/2, 2/4, 3/6, 4/8, and 5/10. Of course, some 20/40 games play like 5/10 games, and some 5/10 games play like 50/100 games. Getting a feel for your opponents is important when you consider your starting hand requirements. (See Chapter Seven "Psyching Your Opponents" for more information on this subject. A discussion about starting hand selection for no-limit play is included in the advanced strategy section beginning on page 15.)

Early Position

The following hands are recommended in early position (seats three, four and five):

AA—A pair of aces (hole cards often called pocket rockets) is the best starting hand in any form of Texas Hold'em. Unless you are a seasoned professional, it is recommended to always enter the pot with a raise when you hold a pair of aces. If you raise and are reraised, raise again. This does two things that are favorable for you: It gets as much money as possible into the pot, and it will often force small drawing hands, such as suited connectors (for example ♠4-♠5) and small pairs to fold before the flop. Your goal with pocket rockets is to play either heads-up (against only one opponent) or, at the most, against two opponents. Three or more opponents greatly reduce your chances of winning a hand, even if you have the best starting hand.

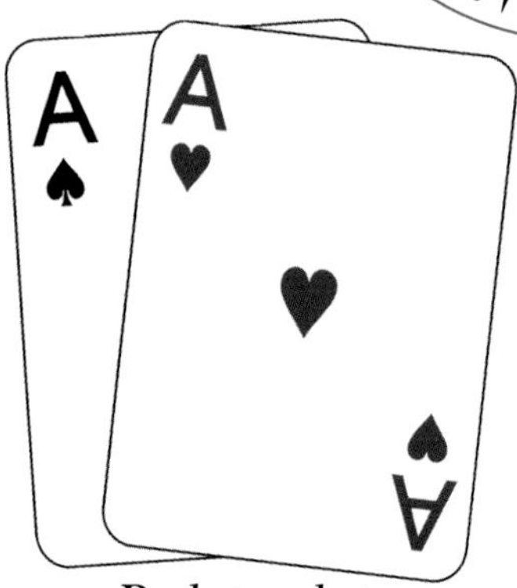

Pocket rockets

KK—A pair of kings (often called cowboys) is the second best starting hand in Texas Hold'em. Just like pocket aces, you should always raise with pocket kings when you enter a pot. Your goals are the same as with pocket aces with the additional goal of hoping to force out opponents who hold an ace with a small kicker. With pocket kings, any flop that contains an ace can be dangerous to you since many low-limit players play any hand containing an ace.

AKs and AK—The third best starting hand in Texas Hold'em is AK whether suited or not. This is one hand that has a rule that is set in stone: You must raise before the flop with AK. You must force as many opponents as possible to fold before the flop when you hold AK. This is a drawing hand and must be protected. Drawing hands must almost always improve to win. Made hands, such as high pairs like AA,

KK, and QQ will often win even if they don't improve. Of course, you hope to see at least an A or K on the flop whenever you hold AK. An additional benefit of raising before the flop is that even if you don't hit an ace or king on the flop, your opponents will often respect your pre-flop raise. They will let you see the turn for free by checking after the flop to see what you are going to do.

QQ—Pocket queens are a strong starting hand. Some players may enter the pot with a raise and sometimes they will just limp in (call) to see the flop. This is a double-edged sword. You may raise to force out opponents holding an ace with a small kicker or opponents who like to play a king with a suited kicker, or you may limp in and hope that neither an ace nor king is in the flop so you can win extra bets from the above-mentioned opponents. How you play pocket queens depends on how well you know your opponents' playing styles and on your position. If a player holds them in middle or late position and is the first one in the pot, they should almost always enter with a raise. Any time you hold them, and an ace or king hits on the flop, you are probably beat, especially against three or more opponents.

JJ—Pocket jacks can be dangerous to inexperienced players. Because they look good before the flop, many players enter with a raise. The problem is that any ace, king, or queen on the flop forces you to play defensively, and if you face more than one opponent, you are likely to lose. For this reason, unless you think you can isolate an opponent (discussed in the advanced strategy section beginning on page 15), you should limp in with pocket jacks. Try to look at pocket jacks the same as any other pair below queens: as a drawing hand. Of course, if the flop brings nothing higher than a ten, you should bet aggressively until you're convinced that someone has a better hand.

AQs, AQ, AJs, KQs—These hands should be played from any position, even calling a single raise before the flop. The exception is if a very tight and strong player raises from under-the-gun, then you should consider folding. You should fold everything except AA, KK, and AK if a tight player raises and is reraised before the betting gets to you. Otherwise, these hands are very strong. When you do hit one of your cards on the flop, opponents will often bet as well (give you action) while holding a smaller kicker. This is the best situation to be in. This is why solid players rarely play aces with kickers below a T, especially from early position.

AJ, ATs, KQ, KJs—Depending on the ability of your opponents, you should often fold these hands when you're under-the-gun. You can play them from the fifth position and sometimes from fourth position. These hands are strong, but sometimes an opponent will have a higher kicker when the flop hits you.

Middle Position

The following hands are recommended in middle position (seats six and seven):

TT, 99, AT, KJ, QJs—These are drawing hands and will almost always need to improve to win. You should rarely call a raise with these hands. With the pairs (TT and 99), you are hoping to flop a set (three of a kind, also called trips). The other three hands can and do win

when the flop hits you, but even if you have the top pair after the flop, you may not have the top kicker. With these hands, you should often bet after the flop if you do hit something in order to get an idea of where you are in the hand. If you bet and are reraised, depending on the opponent, you will usually lose. Often though, this bet after the flop will win the hand, and even if it doesn't, it can set up a bluffing opportunity on the turn.

Late Position

The following hands are recommended in late position (seats eight, nine, and ten).

88, 77, 66, 55, 44, 33, 22—Your main hope is to flop a set with these pairs. As with all of the hands here and below, you should rarely call a raise from a solid player. As discussed in Chapter Six "Do the Math!," most drawing hands prefer to have many opponents so that when you hit your draw, you will be able to collect more than enough money to pay for the times you don't.

KT, QJ—These two hands usually need to end up being part of a straight, two pairs, or trips (three of a kind) to win a very big pot. If there are a lot of opponents in the pot in front of you, and if you do hit a pair on the flop, there is a good chance you will be out-kicked (an opponent has a better kicker). For this reason, don't rely too heavily on them just because they are face cards (kings, queens, and jacks are called face cards). Fold them if the action has been raised and reraised in front of you.

A9s, A8s, A7s, A6s, A5s, A4s, A3s, A2s, K9s, QTs, JTs—With these hands you are hoping to flop a flush or flush draw. Rarely play these in any position except the button. Note that often the A9s through A6s are not as strong as A5s, A4s, A3s, and A2s since the latter can be part of a straight.

Small Blind

The small blind is a unique situation in that you already have half a bet in the pot. This means that you can see the flop for a discounted price. For this reason, you will see the flop in an unraised pot with any of the above hands and QT, JT, K8s, K7s, K6s, K5s, K4s, K3s, and K2s from the small blind. As in a few of the recommended hands above with the suited cards, you are hoping to flop a flush or flush draw; and with the QT and JT a straight, straight draw, two pairs, or trips.

This is a good time to discuss the blinds. Once you have posted a blind, the money is no longer yours. Many players feel that because they have money in the pot, they must protect their blind. This thinking will often lead to playing far weaker hands than your opponents, and basically you will be throwing good money after bad. An example of this is if you are in the big blind and hold 2/7 unsuited. This is the worst possible starting hand. If the post is raised before you can act, you must fold. In a raised pot, you have such a minuscule chance of winning the hand with 2/7 that putting any more money in

A 2 and a 7 unsuited are the worst possible hole cards.

the pot will most often be costly. Another way to look at this is even if you had the opportunity to see the flop for free, you will rarely win a pot holding a hand as weak as 2/7.

You can also be psychologically trapped if the flop gives you a pair on one of your cards. Now because you have a pair, you want to stay in the game, so you continue to throw money into the pot. In all probability, however, another player has your pair with a higher kicker because most players would not call the big blind with two low cards. If you hit two pairs, trips, or even a full house, the probability of winning increases to the point where it would be worthwhile to continue, but the possibility of losing always looms.

It's easy for most players to release the worst possible hole cards when the prospect of winning is low, but what if your hole cards are J9 at the small blind, you call, and a J or an 8 and a 7 are flopped? You have a pair and you have a chance at an inside straight. These types of hands can make you a loser in the long run if you stay with them against strong players. Remember, after the flop, you will be the first to bet—the worst possible position, so you have that against you as well. Using this same reasoning, don't call the half bet in the small blind without a decent starting hand.

Big Blind

When you are in the big blind, you will often have the opportunity to check and see the flop for free. This is usually a good play, especially if you hold a hand not mentioned above. There are, however, a few hands that you should raise with in the big blind. AA, KK, AKs, and AK should all be brought in with a raise to build the pot. An exception is if only one or two players have entered the pot, you may check with AA and KK in order to disguise your hand and give your opponents an opportunity to hit something on the flop. This can be dangerous because sometimes an opponent who limps in with a small pair may hit a set on the flop.

In this section we discussed the most important concept in becoming and staying a winning Hold'em player—starting hand selection. The hands listed are not the only hands you will ever play in Hold'em. As you gain experience and learn how certain opponents play and learn to read different situations, you will be able to play many different hands many different ways. The important thing is to give yourself a fair chance to win or at least break even while gaining experience. If you are dedicated to following the guidelines, you will be well on your way to becoming a successful Hold'em player.

Advanced Strategy

This section is designed for the player who has some experience at Texas Hold'em and wants to take the next step. Specific strategies and tactics are discussed for advanced starting hand requirements, play after the flop, play on the turn, play on the river, flopping a monster, stealing the blinds, stealing the button, raising, isolating an opponent, bluffing, and player categories, as well as a short discussion on no-limit Hold'em.

Advanced Starting Hand Requirements

In the game of Texas Hold'em, many different factors influence almost everything you do.

Some are facts, and some are educated guesses. One of the most influential considerations in a Hold'em game is how your opponents play. Their playing style should cause you to adjust your starting hand requirements. Here are two examples—both extreme—to illustrate this point.

Example 1: Somehow you find yourself playing Hold'em with Doyle Brunson, Phil Ivey, Howard Lederer, Phil Hellmuth, Gus Hansen, Johnny Chan, Daniel Negreanu, T.J. Cloutier, and Chip Reese. These nine players are arguably the best poker players in the world. Basically, you have no chance to beat them in this game in the long run.

Your starting hand requirements should be significantly tighter than your normal selections. You should probably play nothing worse than a pair of tens in this game because you know that all of these players can outplay you after the flop. When you enter a hand, you want to know that you have one of the best hands, if not the best hand, going into the flop. (As a side note, it is recommended that you respectfully ask each person at the table for an autograph and then run to any other game in the card room if you find yourself in this situation. If, however, you can afford to play in this game and can keep the discipline to play only better than average starting hands, the knowledge that can be gained from these types of players will be invaluable.) This game is a tight/aggressive game, filled with outstanding players, and is the least profitable situation to be in.

Example 2: You are playing with nine tipsy college kids who are practically telling you what their hands are after the flop through their actions. Every time you are beat after the flop, you lay down your hand because you can tell by their actions that they have stronger hands, and every time you have the best hand, they pay you off by calling all your bets until the end. In this game, you can loosen up your starting hand requirements because you always have a good idea where you stand and can collect the maximum amount with your good hands. This is what is usually called a loose/passive game and can be the most profitable situation to be in.

As you can see, the way your opponents play is something you should always be aware of. In addition, starting-hand selection is not the only area of your game that this will force you to modify.

Play After the Flop

How you decide to play a hand after the flop depends on what you have and what you may end up with after the last two community cards are in play. It also depends on how many other players are still in the hand, how they play, and your position and table image. If you have nothing on the flop and it looks as though you won't win even if you hit part of your hand on the turn or river cards, your best option is to check or fold to a bet. For example: You have ♣K-♥Q, and the flop comes ♦A-♦3-♠6. In all likelihood, at least one of your opponents has an ace, and it is possible one of them has two diamonds. Even if a king or queen hits on the turn or river, you probably will not win the hand. This should be an easy fold to any bet.

What do you do if you hit part of the flop? Let's use the same starting hand as above:

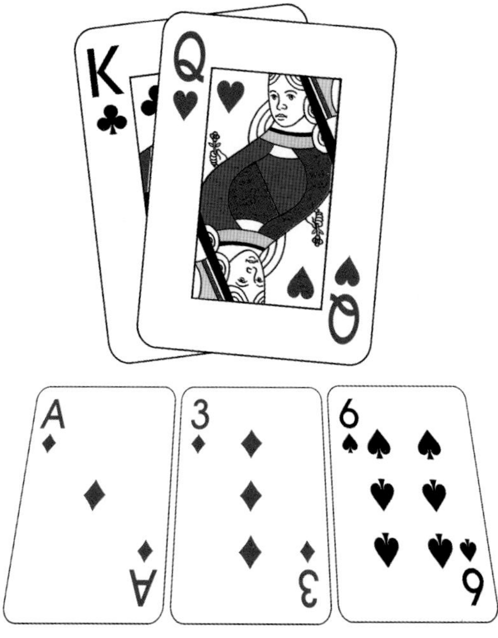

Drop this hand to a bet.

(♣K-♥Q) with a flop of ♠T-♦J-♣6. You have flopped an open-ended straight draw and hold two over cards ("over" refers to cards in hands that are higher than the highest card on the

Bet this hand.

table). Any ace or nine will give you the best hand (a straight), and any king or queen may give you top pair.

Note that if a king or queen does come, it may give one of your opponents a straight or a pair with a higher kicker. Nevertheless, this is a perfect opportunity for a semibluff. You may get an opponent with a better hand (say a pair of nines) before the turn to fold. In addition, even if your bet is called, you have an excellent chance to improve to the best hand. Another example is if the flop is ♣A-♣Q-♥7. You have middle pair (which could be the best hand) with a backdoor flush draw and a backdoor straight draw. In this situation, checking and calling one bet to see what the turn brings is recommended.

One last example: You have middle pair with nothing else from a flop of ♠A-♦K-♥8. Player A will often bet into this flop to see where he/she is. If another opponent reraises, Player A often folds unless that opponent is a very loose player, and Player A is in position. If, however, you are last to act and it is checked to you, take a free look at the turn to see if your hand improves.

Checking to see the turn for free, however, may not always be the best play. The other option is to raise. Often when you raise in this situation, no matter what comes on the turn, your opponents will check to the raiser (you), and you can see the river for free. The added advantage is that it only costs you a small bet because you bet before the minimum bet doubles on the turn. Good poker players are aware of this advanced play and sometimes use it.

Now let's take a look at those situations where you hit the flop. In most low-limit

Hold'em games, fancy plays, such as check raising and slow playing, fail to gain much, if any, advantage. For this reason it is recommended to bet when you think you have the best hand. Continuing with the example below: Your hole cards are ♣K-♥Q, and the flop is ♥K-♦8-♣6.

Bet this hand.

You have top pair with a good kicker. If you are first to act, bet. If someone bets into you, raise. Only if a solid player reraises you should you consider folding this hand. The only hands that are ahead of you at this time are trips or a player that had AK in the hole. If the player who reraises you raised before the flop, he/she may hold AK, but if there was no preflop raise, it is unlikely anyone holds AK.

The times that you hit a really big hand on the flop give you the opportunity to play a few different ways. In most low-limit games, it is best just to bet every chance you get as someone holding the second best hand will pay you off by calling you through the river. If, however, you hit a monster (great hand) and there are two or more opponents still in the hand, you may be able to extract extra bets if you play correctly. As in most situations, it pays to know how your opponents play. Let's look at a situation and technique that can win you extra bets with your best hands.

Let's say you hold a pair of nines and the flop is A, A, 9. You have flopped a full house, and it is likely that one of your opponents holds an ace for trips. Many times in this situation it is correct to check or call instead of raising on the flop. For one thing, if none of your opponents holds an ace, whenever you bet, they will all fold unless they are very poor players. If you check on the flop and everyone checks behind you, just bet on the turn. You have lost nothing, and possibly someone has picked up a draw to a second best hand. If someone bets into you and there are players behind you, by just calling instead of raising, the players behind you may call the single bet but may fold if you raise. In this situation, the player who bet into you will almost always bet into you on the turn because you showed weakness by just calling on the flop instead of raising. After a bet on the turn, you can either raise, or if you are fairly certain of a bet on the river, just call, and then raise on the river. Remember that the bets on the turn and the river are twice what they are on the flop.

Play on the Turn

Most of the time, the way you play your hand on the turn should be straightforward. Your hand is well defined because you can see six out of the seven cards that you will be able to

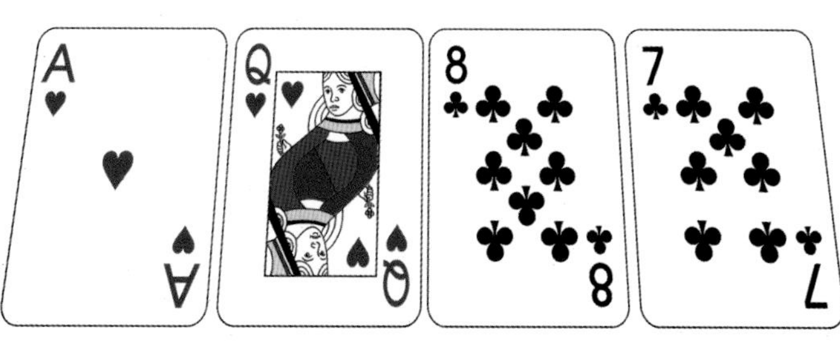

You hold top two pairs.

use. It is easy to see if there are any possible flushes or flush draws, straights or straight draws. Note that most straights are made when high cards are on the board since more players play two face cards than two small cards (unless they are playing low-suited connectors, such as ♦6-♦7).

Here are some questions to ask yourself when deciding how to play on the turn. Do I have the best hand? If I hit the draw, will the draw make my hand the best possible hand? If I have the best hand now, what cards can come on the river that will beat me?

One very important thing to remember is when you have the best hand—but a miracle card on the river can beat you—don't let your opponent draw to it for free. This may sound like a contradiction to the advice above about maximizing your winnings with a strong hand, but it's not. You should check in order to draw more bets only when you have a completely unbeatable or almost unbeatable hand. If, however, when you have the best hand, but the board is scary in that a miracle card can beat you, you must bet. For example: You hold ♦A-♠Q and the board shows ♥A-♥Q-♣8-♣7.

You hold the top two pairs and probably have the best hand at this point. Any heart or club, however, could give one of your opponents a flush to beat you, or another high card could give another opponent a straight. You must bet into this board so your opponents won't see the river for free. We will discuss this situation further in Chapter Six "Do the Math!," but for now you are a favorite against any flush or straight draw in this situation. To be a winning player, your goal is to get money into the pot in situations where you are a favorite over and over again. While it is true that occasionally your opponent will hit the card he/she needs to beat you, over the long run your wins and losses in these situations will follow the odds and make you a winner.

Play on the River

With one exception, which will be discussed shortly, when you believe you have the best hand on the river, you should bet and/or raise. Low-limit Hold'em is full of players who will consistently call with second, third, and even fourth best hands because they are afraid of getting bluffed out of a pot. Until you have thousands of hands worth of experience, don't get fancy on the river. Just bet your best hands, and check when you aren't sure. If you check and there is a bet behind you, even if you

think that you are likely beat, it may still be correct to call. This involves pot odds, which is discussed in Chapter Six.

Now, an explanation on the exception mentioned above. If you know a player will try to bluff you on the river, you should check, and when he/she bets, you should raise. This is called a check-raise and can be a powerful tactic. The important word in the above sentence is "know." If you're not at least 90 percent sure that he/she will bet, you should go ahead and bet. Some players always bet on the river. Once again, pay attention to how your opponents play, and you will be far ahead of most recreational players. The biggest mistake new players make involving the check-raise is that many of them become too fond with using it, thus giving up bets trying to do it. There is always a chance that the player behind you will check, when that player would have called a bet.

Flopping a Monster

The term "flopping a monster" means that the flop fits your hand perfectly. For example: Your hole cards are ♥8-♥9 and the flop comes ♥T-♥J-♥7 to give you a straight flush.

Because these kinds of flops are extremely rare, not too much time will be spent discussing these situations, but you should have an idea on how to extract the most money from your opponents when you have a monster. Seasoned players always check or just call when they have a monster and someone else bets on the turn. The hope is that someone will bet into you on both the flop and the turn. If everyone checks on the flop, the card that comes on the turn may give someone a

Straight flush

second best hand, and hopefully they will pay you off. Note that in order for checking to be the correct play, there should not be any cards that can come on the turn that you would fear. In the above example, even if the ♥Q hits on the turn, an opponent would have had to start with ♥A-♥K to have you beat. If this does occur, you would have to pay them off because the odds of this happening are so slim. In a perfect world, one of your opponents will bet into you on the river, you will call, and one will call behind you.

The reasons you don't raise on the flop are twofold: You want as many people to call as possible to maximize the pot, and—because the bets double on the turn—any raising should be done on the turn or the river. If there are players who act behind you, you should call only on the turn if you are bet into. If one of the players behind you raises and the

opponent in front calls the raise on the turn, then you can go ahead and reraise. Your hopes are that at least one of your opponents will hit a second best hand and cap the betting on the river and even on the turn—if you are lucky.

Stealing the Blinds

Stealing the blinds or attempting to steal the blinds is when a player in late position, often the button, is the first one to enter the pot and raises with the hope of the blinds folding to the raise. For this to work, you must study your opponents and know how they play. Some players will defend their blinds by always calling a raise. Obviously you can't steal their blind if this is the way they play.

Stealing the blinds happens much more in no-limit Hold'em than in limit Hold'em because you can make a large enough raise in no-limit to often drive the blinds out of the hand. Unless the blinds are extremely tight, I don't recommend trying to steal blinds very often without a solid hand. Moreover, since many players attempt to steal blinds from the button, most players don't respect a raise from this position and will call with marginal hands. For this reason, experienced players like to try a steal occasionally from one seat to the right of the button.

Stealing the Button

As previously discussed, being last to act is a great advantage in Hold'em. Stealing the button is when a player in middle to late position enters the pot with a raise hoping to force the players between him/her and the blinds to fold. Once again, observe your opponents in order to have an idea if this can work.

By this time you may be tired of reading that you must study your opponents. Nonetheless, to be a top-level poker player it is a skill you must continually develop.

Raising

There are only two reasons to raise in Hold'em: You raise to build the pot, or you raise to reduce the field against you by forcing opponents to fold. A good example of raising to reduce the field is when many players see the flop and you hit the second or third best pair with a chance to draw to a better hand. For example: You hold ♦K-♦J and the flop is ♦Q-♥J-♦3.

You have a middle pair with a flush draw and a straight draw.

You have a middle pair with a draw to a flush and a backdoor draw to a straight (that is, two draws to make the straight). You should

always bet into this hand if many players want to see the flop and you are the first player to act. Occasionally you may win the hand at this time because all your opponents fold, but often players holding a queen or better will call in this situation. Others will fold because you are showing strength by betting. If you are raised, this usually means someone has a set or top pair with a good kicker. When you are raised, it is almost always correct to call the raise since there are many cards that can help you, such as any diamond, any jack, or any king.

A situation in which you are raising to build the pot is when you believe you have the best hand and a player bets into you, you call, a player behind you raises, and the first player calls. You can raise in this position, and most of the time both opponents will call your raise because they have invested two bets.

Isolating an Opponent

One reason to reduce the field with a raise is to isolate an opponent. By raising at a particular time, you may get everyone to fold with the exception of one opponent. The ideal opportunity to do this is when an opponent raises the big blind before anyone calls and you are the next person to act. Your reraise will often force everyone else to fold, thus isolating the initial raiser. This creates three advantages for you: You have position; you are playing heads-up; and you have shown strength. Do this if you have a strong hand and/or you feel you can outplay your opponent after the flop.

Bluffing

Bluffing is when you bet with an inferior hand hoping to cause your opponents to fold. There are very few good opportunities in low-limit Hold'em to bluff. Players at that level will call with almost anything because they are afraid to be bluffed out of a hand, and they populate low-limit Hold'em. As you advance to higher limits, including no-limit Hold'em, bluffing becomes an important weapon in a good player's arsenal.

What is most important for a beginning player to know about bluffing is that it is practically impossible to bluff more than two opponents out of a hand. There are, however, two bluffing situations that can improve your game: the semibluff and bluffing when a scare card hits.

A semibluff is betting into a pot when you don't know if you have the best hand but have a chance to improve to the best hand. For example: Your hole cards are ♥J-♥T and the flop is ♣T-♥8-♥7.

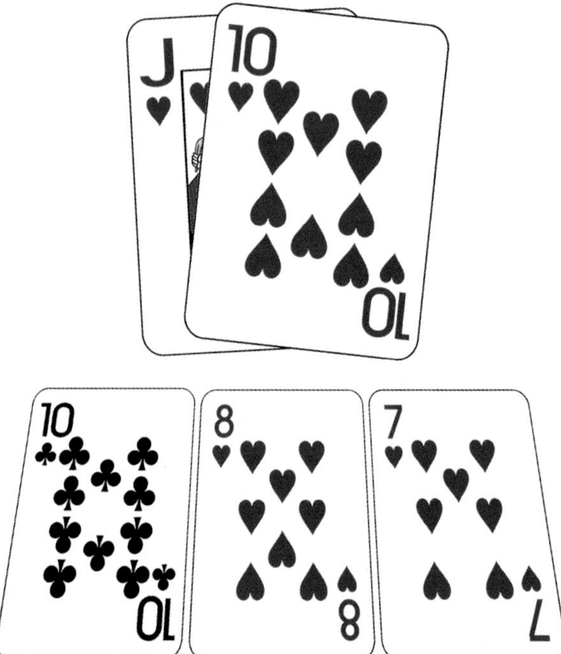

Semibluff with a pair of tens and several draws.

It is recommended that you bet into this pot as a semibluff. You have second pair (a pair of tens) and could be behind in the hand to a straight, a set, or a pair of jacks. The important thing to remember is that you can improve to a flush, straight, trips, or two pair on the turn or river. Your bet in this situation can result in four outcomes with three of them being good for you:

- Everyone may fold, and you win the hand.
- All but one or two opponents may fold, eliminating some drawing hands.
- An opponent may reraise your bet.
- All of your opponents may call.

The only result that is not immediately beneficial to you is the fourth one—everyone calls (often called "flat calling"). Of course, if everyone folds, you win the pot. Eliminating opponents or reducing the field is also beneficial to your hand. You may be asking why being reraised in this situation is a good thing. The reraise provides you with a tremendous amount of information. Unless you are playing with a very loose player who raises every time he/she plays a hand, you are almost always beat at this time if you are reraised. This means that you now know that in order to win the hand you will have to improve on the turn or the river. You will use this information to decide if you want to call the reraise and also how to play your hand on the turn and the river.

As will be discussed in Chapter Six, it is almost always correct in limit Hold'em to call this reraise. The reason that flat calling is not a good outcome is you gain no further information. It does have a silver lining, for it builds the pot for the times that you do hit your hand on the turn.

Remember the discussion about maximizing your winnings; that is, call with the best hand (especially with a monster) in this situation in order to maximize the pot and save the raising until the turn when the bet size doubles. Making plays like these and realizing that your opponents, at least the good ones, are capable of making these plays will separate you from the average poker player. Many times it is correct to bet into a pot to gain information in this way. As you advance in skill level, you may even raise an opponent who bets into you on the flop as a semibluff to find out how good his/her hand is and possibly set up a bluff on the turn or river by showing strength. This play is not for beginners because it can cost you a large amount of money. So don't use it regularly until you have many hours of experience.

Bluffing when a scare card hits is another advanced play that many professionals use, especially in no-limit Hold'em. There is one rule that should always be followed when using this play: Never try it with more than one opponent in the hand. The chance of success is so small against two or more opponents that it will cost you money in the long run. Here's an example: Your hole cards are ♣A-♠T and the flop is ♥T-♦K-♣4. The turn brings the ♣6.

At this point you may have the best hand, but you may be up against a pair of kings or better. If any club hits on the river, this can be a good time to bluff. The club on the river makes a flush possible, and if you bet on the

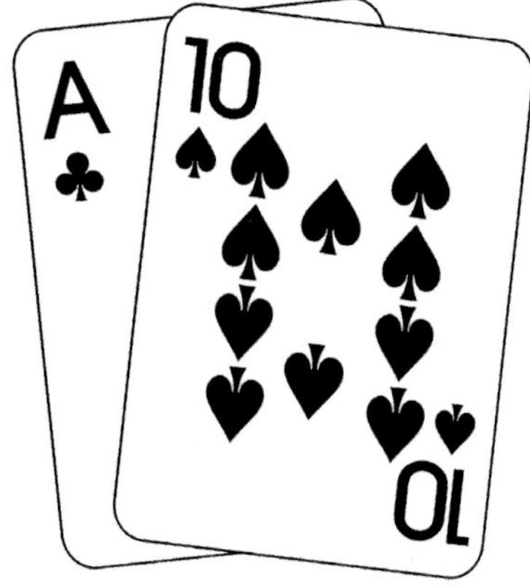

The ♣6 is the scare card.

river, you are representing that you hit it. Notice that you have the ace of clubs, so even if your opponent has two clubs, he/she knows that you could have a higher flush. Also, an opponent holding a king is not happy to see the possible flush on the board. Another reason this is a good time to try this is that only one of the clubs was on the flop, so an opponent who started with two clubs probably folded his/her hand if they didn't have any other draws.

It is important to remember how the hand was played out because if everyone checked on the flop, a player holding two clubs got a free look at the turn. This is an example of why betting into the flop as a semibluff is often correct. In this hand, if you had bet into the flop, any opponent holding two clubs with no other draws should have folded. Of course, in some low-limit Hold'em games, your opponents won't fold when they are supposed to. This is why you should never try this tactic against more than one opponent. When you do use it, you should be certain that your opponent is capable of folding if a scare card hits. Some players will never fold in this situation, and if you can identify them, you will save money by not trying to bluff them.

Player Categories

Because the way players play is important, it is helpful to place them into categories. Some players find that by attaching names with categories it helps them recall how each opponent plays. Here is a list of different playing styles followed by suggested names for each type of player. It is important to remember that any player may change from one playing session to the next and that some players can even change within a playing session. A poor player may improve over time, and a good player may be having a bad day. Therefore, it is a good idea to use the beginning of each session to re-evaluate any familiar opponents while you evaluate new ones.

• **Tight/Aggressive**—You should strive to become this type of player. Tight/aggressive players don't play many hands, but when they do play a hand, it is played very aggressively. They often enter the pot with a raise and will push the action by betting and raising until shown that they are beat. Every time a player bets or raises, it forces other players to make decisions, and whenever players must make a decision, they may make a mistake. Tight/aggressive players capitalize on this tactic by providing opportunities for their

opponents to make these mistakes. The name assigned to these players is "Solid." Experienced players usually respect their bets and raises because they seldom enter a pot with a poor hand. Meanwhile, solid players are capable of folding a good hand if they are convinced they are beat. When a solid player is quiet and constantly observing everything at the table while using the advanced strategies discussed before, the name assigned to them is "Professional." A game with too many solid and/or professional players is not a good game to be in.

• **Loose/Aggressive—**Loose/aggressive players play too many hands, usually raise, and are very difficult to bluff. These players can be dangerous because it is often difficult to guess what their hole cards are (often called putting them on a hand). Thus you are seldom certain where you stand in a hand with them. For this reason it is important to keep your starting hand requirements tight so you are often in the hand with better cards than loose/aggressive players. Most loose/aggressive players try to play the correct way, which is tight/aggressive, but they simply play too many hands. At times loose/aggressive players have long winning streaks because like tight/aggressive players, they force their opponents to make decisions and mistakes. The problem is in the long run, loose/aggressive players will be losing players because of their starting hand selection. Many good poker players—referred to as "solid"—will at times slip into loose/aggressive play by lowering their starting hand requirements. Most of these players correct this in time, but it is something to keep an eye out for, especially if they are not having a good session. The name assigned to the loose/aggressive player is "Overly Zealous." The overly zealous play many hands and always raise if they are in a hand. A true overly zealous is impossible to put on a hand since he/she can and will play anything. Thus they are very dangerous in the short run. In the long run, a solid player will end up with all of the overly zealous's money as long as the solid player can survive the short-term financial swings.

• **Tight/Weak—**Tight/weak players usually have a fairly good idea of proper starting hand selection and stick to it. They rarely raise unless they have the absolute best hand, and they prefer to check and call to see what is coming next. The biggest problem with this type of play is that tight/weak players rarely protect their hand (by betting or raising to narrow the field) and are often beat by a player who hits a draw or miracle card. Tight/weak players may show a small profit in

TEXAS DOLLY

Arguably the best living poker player and probably the best Hold'em player ever is Doyle Brunson, nicknamed "Texas Dolly." He has won nine World Series of Poker events and many other tournaments, has written poker books, and is still going strong. Born in Longworth, Texas, in 1933, Brunson was such a good athlete that an NBA team drafted him when he finished college. A knee injury kept him from playing, and he turned to poker. Often credited as the single most important individual in the growth of poker, Doyle Brunson is truly a legend.

games full of poor players because of their proper starting hand selection, but solid players will run over tight/weak players. The tight/weak players are called "Semi-Weak."

• **Loose/Weak**—Loose/weak players do all the wrong things while playing poker. They play too many hands. They check and call when they should raise. And they always call on the river with second, third, and often worse hands. These players are referred to as "Calling Stations." Poker players call them "Fish." Calling stations will always pay off your good hands, and you should often try to isolate them to take advantage of their weak play.

No-Limit Hold'em Advanced Strategy

At one time no-limit Hold'em was offered only in tournament settings, but it has recently been offered in many card rooms as a regular ring game. Since the strategy for tournament play is discussed in Chapter Ten, no-limit ring game strategy is discussed here.

Most no-limit ring games have a set buy-in (for instance, $200) or a range of buy-ins (for instance, your buy-in might be for any amount between $200 and $400). Of course, if you lose all of your chips, you can buy back in. The games have a blind structure and minimum betting structure just like regular limit games. A game may be called $200, 1/2 no-limit, which means that the buy-in is $200, the blinds are .50 and $1, and the minimum bet the first two rounds is $1 and the last two rounds is $2. In Chapter Eleven, you'll learn how much money you should have available to handle the swings involved in playing poker. The recommendations in that chapter are based on limit play, not no-limit. Because of the structure of no-limit, upswings and downswings are magnified. For this reason, if you decide to play no-limit Hold'em, you may need a larger bankroll—especially to start with—than the recommendations in Chapter Eleven.

No-limit ring games like these can be profitable for the better players. A strong recommendation is to play extremely tight when you first sit at a table until you get a feel for your opponents. These games allow solid players to use all of their tools in areas such as bluffing, pot odds, psychology, and solid game skills. Drawing hands go down in value and made hands (such as pocket pairs) go up.

You will learn in Chapter Six the importance of pot odds and how to use them. For players who have a solid understanding of pot odds, no-limit Hold'em can be a gold mine. Because of the ability to place any size bet, you can manipulate pot odds to force your opponents to pay too high of a price to draw to their hand or make the price low enough that it is correct for them to call when you want them to. This fact alone makes the understanding of the correct use of pot odds imperative to anyone hoping to be a successful poker player.

Tight/aggressive play is the only way to be a successful no-limit Hold'em player. Good players rarely call in no-limit. They almost always fold or raise. This doesn't mean that you should never call; it just means that as you gain experience, rarely will you find yourself behind at the beginning of a hand. Instead, you allow your opponents opportunities to make mistakes because of this aggressive style

of play combined with tight starting hand requirements.

While playing no-limit Hold'em, your first instinct will probably be to move all-in when you see pocket aces. In a typical game, this will win you the pot, but you will likely win only the blinds since everyone else probably folded. When you have a great starting hand such as AA, KK, AK, or QQ, your goal should be to raise enough to make all but one or two opponents fold. Then, if you are reraised before the flop, you can move all-in. Winning the most pots in a session is nice, but winning the most money is what counts. For this reason you must consider how to maximize your winnings with your best hands. The strategies concerning checking, raising, and check-raising are all tools you can use to make money at the poker table.

QUESTIONS

1. What are the best starting hole cards in Texas Hold'em?
2. When you move up in stakes (play higher limit games), as a general rule are your opponents better? Are they tighter?
3. What hands should you always raise with before the flop, no matter what position you are in?
4. If you are in a game with many good players and are first to act with TT, should you call, raise, or fold?

5. In the same tight game as above, you are on the button and hold KK while the first player to act raised the big blind and everyone else folded. What should you do?

(Answers are on page 60.)

Chapter Three

OMAHA: TO SPLIT OR NOT TO SPLIT

The key to winning at Omaha is a solid understanding of the rules. If you are looking to win, you've found the right chapter.

As in most forms of poker, the majority of a good player's profit comes from the mistakes of opponents. The first step in becoming a profitable player is a thorough understanding of the rules of Omaha high-only and Omaha high-low split (often called Omaha/8). The hi-lo (high-low) version of Omaha will be discussed since it is the more popular of the two versions. Moreover, the high-only version is played exactly the same way as the hi-lo version except the pot is not split and the high hand is awarded the entire pot.

Basic Strategy

Omaha is played at set limit or pot limit (raises can be up to the current size of the pot). Though it is occasionally available, no-limit Omaha is rarely played. In this chapter limit Omaha will be discussed unless it is stated otherwise. It is strongly recommended that you play only limit Omaha until you have a great deal of experience because pot-limit Omaha can be a brutal game for the beginning player and can take a heavy toll on your bankroll. Rarely play pot-limit because, like no-limit, one mistake can be extremely expensive.

Nine or ten players is customary in Omaha high-low split, which has a rotating blind system. Usually a qualification of eight or better is placed on the low hand, and the best high hand will split the pot with the best low hand. This means for a hand to qualify as a low, it must have five cards not paired that are ranked eight or lower. For example, a hand consisting of ace, two, three, seven, and eight qualifies as a low hand; but a hand of ace, two, three, seven, and nine does not.

A wheel is the best possible low hand.

Each player is dealt four down cards, called "hole" cards. Then three community cards are dealt face up in the center of the table. These cards are called the "flop." Another card is dealt face up, which is called the "turn," followed by the last card being dealt face up, called the "river." Rounds of betting are before the flop, after the flop, after the turn, and after the river.

Each player must use exactly three cards from the five community cards and two from

his/her hand in any combination to form a high hand and/or a low hand. The same five cards do not have to be used for the high and the low. Note that if there are not at least three community cards ranked eight or below, there will be no low hand, and the entire pot will be awarded to the best high hand. The two most important rules are: (1) Each player must use exactly three community cards and two hole cards; (2) the order of ranking for low hands is from the highest of the five cards.

The easiest way to rank low hands is to read them backward as a number with the lowest number winning. For example: 2-3-4-6-8 would be read 8-6, 4-3-2 and 3-4-5-6-7 would be read 7-6, 5-4-3, which would be the lower of the two hands. Many times two players will have the same low hand and split the low half of the pot. This is often called "getting quartered."

Omaha/8 games, especially on the Internet, are filled with players who don't know how to play the game. Almost all Omaha/8 players are current or former Texas Hold'em players who use the same thought process and mentality while playing Omaha/8 as when they played Hold'em. This is why Omaha/8 can be profitable. Because there are four hole cards instead of two, many players think they see more possibilities to win and thus play far too many hands.

Another weakness in the games of many players is not folding after the flop when the only hope they have is a split pot or a runner-runner (that is, needing the turn and river cards) to make their hand. In Omaha, after the flop, your hand is well defined. You see 7 out of the 9 cards you will use—almost 80 percent. In contrast, after the flop in Hold'em you have seen only 5 of 7 cards, which is just over 70 percent. Omaha/8 tends to be a much more straightforward and mathematical game than Hold'em. For this reason, Omaha/8 tends to have less short-term variance (luck) than Hold'em. Many players enjoy playing Omaha/8 more than Hold'em because of the reduced variance. The problem is it can sometimes be hard to find a good Omaha/8 game, but there never seems to be a shortage of Hold'em games.

An important skill to master in Omaha/8 is reading the board. You must be able to look at the cards on the board and consider what the best possible hand is, the likelihood of someone having the best hand, how close your hand is to the best hand, and what chance you have to improve to the best hand. As will be discussed shortly, you must often have the best hand possible to win. Reading the board is a skill that will become easier as you gain experience. A good way to improve your skills is to read the board on every hand even when you have folded. This not only will improve your skills but also will help you learn what types of hands your opponents are playing. You need to determine if there is a possible low, if there is a possible flush, if there is a possible straight (which will be possible on most hands), and if there is a possible full house (whenever the board shows one or two pairs, players probably have a full house).

Starting Hand Selection

As in Texas Hold'em, the most important decision you will make in Omaha/8 is which hands to enter a pot and which hands to fold.

Omaha/8 is a game of scoops (winning both the high and low pots on the same hand or the high when no low is possible) and redraws (having a good hand with the opportunity to improve to a better hand with community cards). A hand containing an ace that is suited to another card in the hand is a good example of both scooping and redraw hands. You can win low with the ace, and you can win high with an ace high flush if your three suited cards hit on the board. For these reasons, your starting hand selection should include mostly hands that have the possibility to scoop and that offer redraws. Hands that have an ace are the most common starting hands because an ace can be used for a high hand and a low hand.

Another important concept is having counterfeit protection. For example, let's look at two hands, one with A-2-3-5 and one with A-2-Q-K. If the flop comes 4-6-7, you have the best possible low hand. However, if an A or 2 falls on the turn or river, the hand with A-2-Q-K no longer has the best possible low while the other hand still does. The first hand has counterfeit protection, which is extremely important to Omaha/8 strategy.

This hand has counterfeit protection.

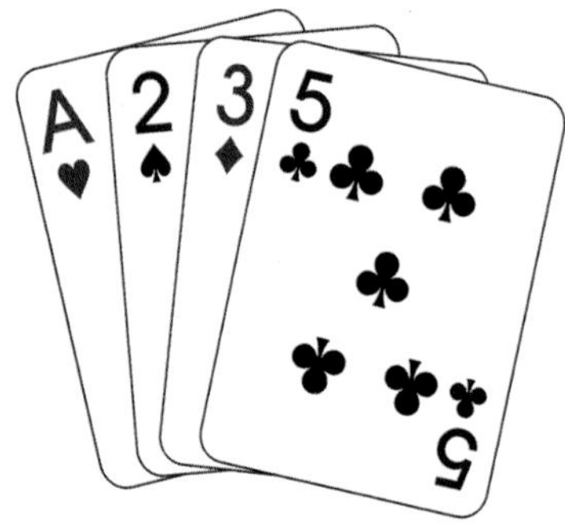

Most experts agree that in Hold'em you should see the flop only about 20 percent of the time. Many players believe because you have four hole cards in Omaha/8 instead of two, you can see more flops. This is only true if you want to be a losing player. The fact is you should see only about 20 percent of the flops in Omaha/8 as well. Starting hand selection is at least as important in Omaha/8 as it is in Hold'em, perhaps even more so.

At the lower limits, position is not nearly as important in Omaha/8 as it is in Hold'em. While it is nice to act last, it can be almost as good to act first, and even acting between players is not as bad as doing so in Hold'em. Due to the more straightforward way Omaha/8 plays and the fact that you should have a very good idea of your chances to win after the flop, you should be able to play almost any hand you decide to play in any position. As you become more experienced and move up in limits, position plays a more important role. Position also plays a larger role in pot-limit Omaha/8 because you may be caught with a drawing hand between two players who are raising the pot back and forth in large chunks.

Particularly at the lower limits where the majority of players see the flop, you will often have to start with the best possible hand to win either the high or the low half of the pot. For example, if a flush is possible, you have almost no chance of winning the high pot unless you can beat a flush as one or more of your opponents will have one. If you have a flush and the board pairs (two cards on the board are the same, like K-K or 2-2), then you have probably lost to a full house. This is one of the reasons it is important to have hands that have both high and low potential.

Looking at low possibilities, most players will play any hand containing an A and a 2. If you

have a low that cannot beat one that has A-2, then you probably won't win the low half of the pot unless the ace or two is counterfeited. If you are playing only toward half of the pot after the flop, it is imperative to draw only to the best possible hand. Losing players will often draw to second and third best hands. So add this rule to the two rules already mentioned, and make a mental list containing the following: Scoops, redraws, and draw to the best hand.

In Hold'em, because you start with only two cards, you have only one combination of two cards. In Omaha, you start with four cards that can create six unique two-card combinations. The best starting hands have all four cards working together. Hands that have three cards working together with one card that doesn't (often called a dangler) are weaker than ones with all four working in conjunction. Here are some examples of starting hands that work together and some that don't.

Hands that work together:

You have the best two low cards (A, 2) with counterfeit protection (4) and the possibility to make a straight–A, 2, 3, 4, 5–or an ace high flush in spades with the ♠A-♠9.

This hand has a low draw (A, 2), and three high draws (ace high flush, king high flush, and straight possibilities with the A, K; K, 9; or A, 2).

Arguably this is the best starting hand in Omaha/8 since you have the three lowest cards, two flush draws—both ace high, a pair of aces, and a wheel possibility.

These cards all work together as any combination of low cards while giving you a straight draw, and if an ace hits the board, you will have the best possible low if a low is possible.

Hands that don't work together:

This hand has almost no low possibilities since the six is too high. There are no flush possibilities and only a straight possibility for a high.

Even if you hit a low, an 8 low almost never wins. If you hit a flush or a straight, either one is too low to win in most cases. This hand has almost nothing going for it.

This hand has a very weak low draw and very little high possibility.

This last example illustrates an important point. Many players might think this hand has great straight potential. While this is true, even if you do hit a straight, it will rarely be the best possible straight, and most of the time it will be because there are three cards 8 and below on the board, which makes a low hand for someone else. So you will be playing for only half the pot, and you will rarely have a lock on that half because your top potential is so low. Do you see why this hand is a dangerous one? If you are playing for only half the pot, make sure you are drawing to the best possible hand.

Here is some specific advice about your starting-hand selections. As you are learning to play Omaha/8, play only the following hands. An x denotes any card of any rank. A w denotes a wheel card (2, 3, 4, or 5). A t denotes a ten through a king (T-J-Q-K).

1. [A 2 x x] You must be careful with just an A-2 and no counterfeit protection.
2. [A 3 x x] Play this hand if the ace is suited to one of your other cards.
3. [A w w x] Play as long as the two wheel cards are not the same, like ♠4-♦4)
4. [w w w w] Play four wheel cards even if you have one pair, but not if you hold two pairs or trips.
5. [A t t t] Play an ace with three high cards, especially if the ace is suited. This is a strong hand, particularly if the board doesn't come up with a possible low.
6. [t t t t] Play four high cards, even with a pair or two pairs. This hand is also a good high-only hand.

These guidelines are extremely tight and are meant to be used while you are learning the game. As you gain experience and learn your opponents' playing styles and hand selection, you can play a few more starting hands. Hands with an A, 3, and two high cards are often playable as well as hands containing an ace suited to one other card that offer flush and straight possibilities and some low potential, such as ♥A-♥4-♦6-♣7.

Beginning Omaha/8 players often overrate pairs, especially pocket aces. Unlike Hold'em, a pair will almost never win a pot. Even trips are often beat by a straight, flush, or full house. Hold'em players who start to play Omaha often not only play a hand like ♠A-♣A-♠7-♦8 but also will raise with it before the flop. This hand is unplayable because it will not win the low even if a low is made and will rarely win even if an ace comes on the board unless the board pairs (making a full house), and the 7 and 8 are almost worthless. So if you are a Hold'em player learning to play Omaha/8, don't fall into the trap of overvaluing pocket pairs because they must improve, sometimes considerably, to win.

Game Selection

If you have the choice of more than one game of Omaha/8 to play in, you should look for these type of games:

1. A game that has over 50 percent of the players seeing most flops. In most poker games, especially Omaha/8 and Hold'em, the player who starts with the best hand will win a higher percentage of the time than any other player. If you follow the starting hand guidelines above, you will be entering the pot with a stronger hand on average than the other players.

2. A game with little or no pre-flop raising. You will learn to prefer a game full of passive players.

Sometimes in a card room it may be difficult to find these games, but if you play on the Internet, these games are plentiful.

Advanced Strategy

Let's look at how you should play Omaha/8 hands during the course of a hand.

Play Before the Flop

As in all forms of poker, there are only two reasons to raise before the flop. You are either trying to build the pot or narrow the field. In low-limit Omaha/8, you will rarely narrow the field by raising. This means that most of the time the only reason to raise before the flop is to build the pot. Some advice has been given that would lead a person to believe it is not a good idea to raise before the flop in Omaha/8. Do not take this advice. It has already been discussed that you should be entering the pot with stronger hands on average than your opponents, so why wouldn't you want a bigger pot when you have a better chance to win than any other opponent? With your strongest hands, like ♠A-♠2-♦3-♣6 or ♠A-♠2-♣3-♣K, it is a good idea to build the pot.

These two hands are strong starters and warrant raises.

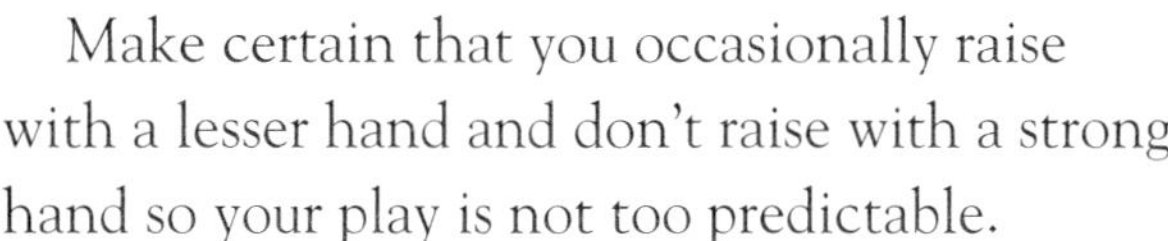

Make certain that you occasionally raise with a lesser hand and don't raise with a strong hand so your play is not too predictable.

Play After the Flop

Your play after the flop should be straightforward. If you have a good hand, bet. If you have a chance to improve to the best hand, check and call if your pot odds are correct (see Chapter Six "Do the Math!"). If the flop didn't help your hand, fold to a bet. This may sound simple, but many players refuse to fold on the flop even when it is obvious they cannot win. Do not become too fond of your starting hand. Unlike Hold'em, even the best starting hand must have some help on the flop in Omaha/8 in order to have a chance to win.

Another problem that many inexperienced Omaha/8 players have is continuing to play after the flop when they have a chance to win only half the pot and it is likely they will have to split their half (thus, being quartered). An example of this is when you hold ♠A-♦2-♥9-♣T, the flop is ♠3-♣6-♦K, and there are three or more players in the pot betting and raising. You have almost no chance at a high hand, and if you do hit a low, it is likely that another player holds an A and a 2. Even worse, if an A or 2 hits on the turn or river, your low will be counterfeited. Continuing to play in situations like these will cost you more money in the long run than they will make for you.

Play on the Turn

Play on the turn is straightforward and simple. If you have the best hand, bet. If you have a draw to the best hand, check and call (once again, assuming the pot odds are correct). If

you have the best possible high or low and a chance at the other (low or high), you should raise to maximize the size of the pot.

Play on the River

Play on the river is the most straightforward situation you will find. If you have the best high hand, raise as much as possible. High hands are almost never quartered. If you are heads-up (against only one opponent) or have three opponents and have the best low hand but no chance at the high hand, it is usually best to just call due to the possibility of being quartered. Realize that against three opponents, if you have the best low hand and are quartered, you will recoup at least every bet you place on the river. When you are against four or more opponents, have the best low hand, and are quartered, you will be making money on every bet you place, so it is often correct to raise. If you are against two opponents and have the best low hand, you should check and call. Sometimes you will be in a hand at the river against two opponents while you have the best low hand and they are both raising. It is extremely likely that you will be quartered in this situation, and you must decide if there is enough money already in the pot to warrant calling all of the raises. Against two opponents, if you have a low and it is quartered, every dollar you put into the pot will return only 75 cents to you.

In some cases, if the pot is small, your best play may be to fold. As you are learning to play, you may never fold in this situation because you want some of that money you contributed to the pot returned to you. Just bear in mind that this can actually cost you money. This is something you will learn with experience.

Epilogue

Omaha/8 can be a fun and profitable game. By mastering the basic concepts in this chapter, you will play better than the average player, and with some experience you should become a consistent winning player.

QUESTIONS

1. What is the best starting hand in Omaha/8?
2. What is counterfeit protection, and why is it important?
3. Are possible flush draws with low-suited cards before the flop more important in Omaha/8 than in Hold'em? Explain why.

Possible flush draw in Omaha.

(Answers are on page 60.)

Chapter Four

STUD HAD ITS DAY

At one time 7-Card Stud dominated the poker world, but today Texas Hold'em has replaced it. This doesn't mean, however, that Stud is dead. Many poker players still prefer it.

For many years, 7-Card Stud was easily the most-played poker game. Then, in the '70s, Texas Hold'em arrived, and it has been gaining popularity during the past decade. It wasn't bad enough that Hold'em became more popular; now Omaha/8 is arguably the second-most-popular poker game. Don't let any of this, however, mislead you into thinking that 7-Card Stud is no longer important to the poker world. It is still offered in most fair-size card rooms, at some tournaments, and is often played by many at home.

Like Omaha, 7-Card Stud is played both high only and high-low (hi-lo), often with an 8 qualifier for the low hand (see Chapter Three). The rules for the hi-lo version have the same basic principles as the hi-lo rules in Omaha. For this reason, the discussion in this chapter will center on the high-only version.

Like both Hold'em and Omaha, 7-Card Stud is played both limit and pot limit. An important difference, however, between Hold'em/Omaha and 7-Card Stud is that Hold'em and Omaha (called flop games) always have community cards, but 7-Card Stud players usually receive their own seven cards (if they stay until the showdown) of which they use five cards to make their best hand. Up to eight players may play in a 7-Card Stud game. It is possible that there will not be enough cards if all eight players make it to the showdown, especially if the dealer burns (discards) a card prior to dealing to the active players. In these infrequent cases, instead of dealing a card to each active player, the dealer turns a "community"card (a card that all active players can use).

Before the deal, each player places an ante into the pot and then receives two down cards (hole cards) and one face up card. The player with the lowest face up card (an ace is high in this situation) is required to start the betting action with the bring-in and must bet at least the required minimum amount. Play continues to the left with either calls, raises, or folds.

After all betting is completed, a fourth card is dealt face up to each player still in the game. From this point on, the player with the highest hand showing starts the action. For example, if the high hand (excluding the hole cards) is a pair after the fourth card is dealt, the player with this pair must check, bet, or fold. Because there is no bring-in requirement after the first betting round, players do not need to fold until there is a bet. Once there is a bet, players left in the game, in turn, must call, raise, or fold. It is possible for players to check around the table, thus having a round with no bets.

A fifth card is dealt face up followed by a betting round, and then a sixth card is dealt face up followed by another round of betting. The seventh card is dealt to each player face down, and the final round of betting starts. Each round is often called a "street" (the third card is called third street, the fourth card is called fourth street, and so on through seventh street).

A skill that is much more important in 7-Card Stud than most other forms of poker is memory. All good 7-Card Stud players remember what cards their opponents were showing before they folded. This is important because players need to know what cards are still out there that can help them and which ones are already gone. Like most forms of poker, other important skills include reading players, reading hands, reading betting patterns, and determining pot odds and starting hand selection.

The best starting hand is two aces in the hole and an ace showing, followed by other three-of-a-kind hands (often called rolled-up trips). Next is a high pair in the hole because it is not only a high pair but also a hidden one. Unlike Omaha/8 where you often must have the best possible starting hand to win, 7-Card Stud plays more like Hold'em when determining the value of your hand. Many pots can be

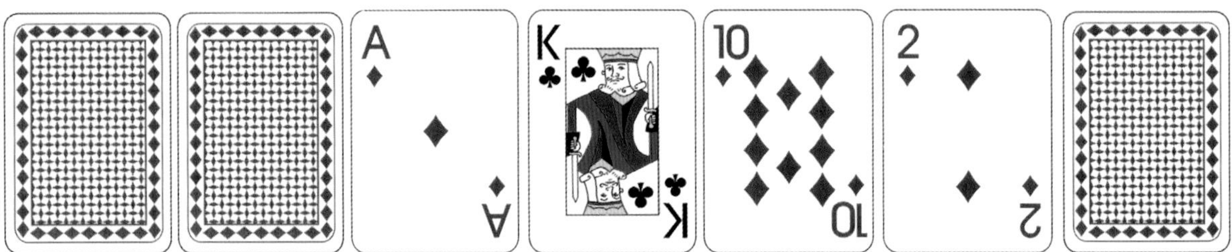

This 7-Card Stud hand could be hiding a flush or a straight.

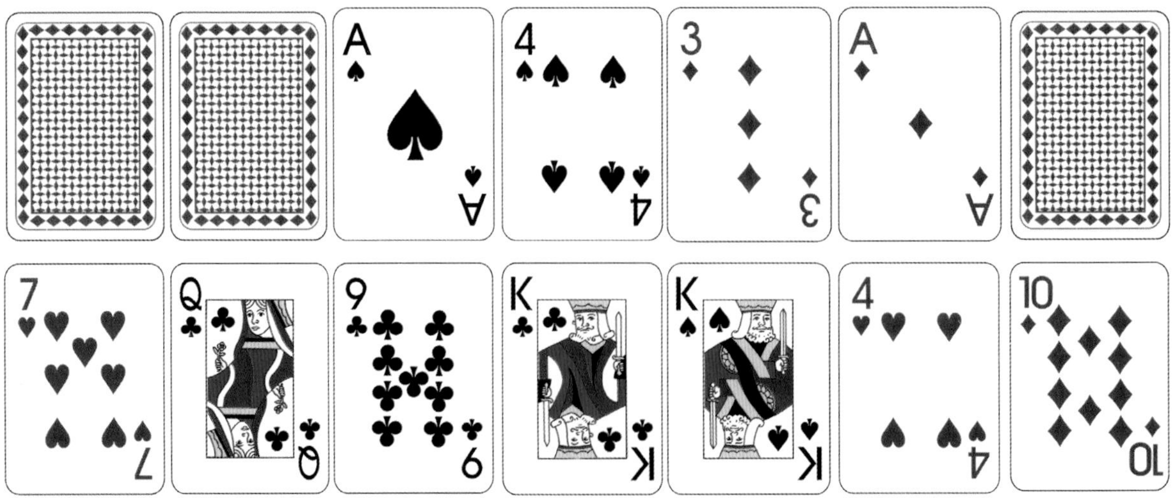

Only by bluffing can the player with kings win.

won with a high pair while trips are very strong. High pairs with one card showing, especially if it is the highest card showing, are also strong starting hands. Hands with strong flush and straight possibilities are also reasonable starting hands.

Like all forms of poker, 7-Card Stud is a game of information. Always be aware of what cards your opponents have showing and what hands they could possibly have. Sometimes you'll notice players who are just learning the game calling bets on the last betting round with hands that can't beat what an opponent has showing. For example, Player A has two aces showing and Player B calls with only a pair of kings. If Player B had simply been paying attention, he/she could have saved at least one bet.

Just like Hold'em and Omaha, the best 7-Card Stud players are tight and aggressive, and they can read players, hands, and situations. Sometimes poor players can win for long stretches of time in Hold'em because of short-term variance, but poor players in 7-Card Stud usually struggle because of a reduced "luck" factor. Understanding what cards are still available to help your hand and pot odds (discussed in Chapter Six) are of the utmost importance to a successful 7-Card Stud player.

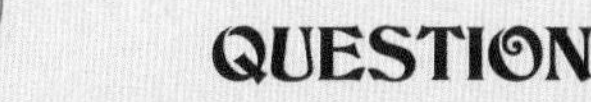

QUESTIONS

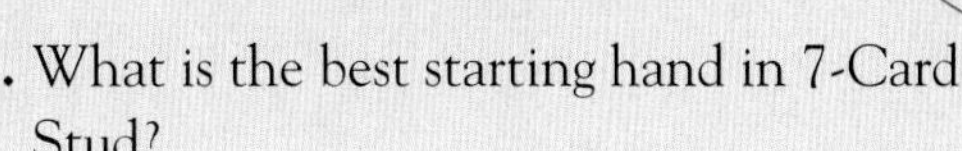

1. What is the best starting hand in 7-Card Stud?

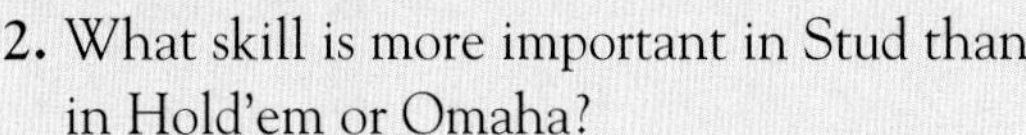

2. What skill is more important in Stud than in Hold'em or Omaha?
3. What should you do at seventh street if you hold two pairs with your highest pair being aces and your opponent has these cards:

(Answers are on pages 60–61.)

Chapter Five

FROM RAZZ TO PINEAPPLE

There are many types of poker games, from old-time favorites to some of the newest twists on Hold'em. Try one of these games at your next poker party.

The number of poker games is countless. In this chapter you will find the rules for poker games other than Texas Hold'em, Omaha, and 7-Card Stud. These games may be hard to find in poker rooms, but if you find one, it may be offered at only one table. The games discussed here are Five-Card Draw, Lowball in Ace-to-Five and Deuce-to-Seven, Razz, Pineapple, and Crazy Pineapple.

Five-Card Draw

Five-card draw is the first poker game that many people learned. Players usually post an ante, receive five cards, and have a round of betting starting to the left of the dealer. Then each player may trade in cards for new ones to improve their hand. This is followed by a second round of betting. It is rarely played in casinos or poker rooms, and it is not played as often as it used to be in home games. For many poker players, its biggest drawback is that it has only two betting rounds.

Lowball

Lowball is a form of draw poker played for the lowest hand. Most Lowball games have a blind structure somewhat like Hold'em while others have an ante. When played with limits (like 5/10), the bet doubles after the draw. Each player receives five cards face down, and play on the first round starts to the left of the big blind with blinds or left of the dealer with antes.

With blinds, each player must call the big blind (some games require the minimum opening bet to be double the big blind), raise, call a raise, reraise, or fold. With antes, each player may check, bet, call the bet, raise, or fold. After this first round of betting, remaining players may trade any number of their cards for new ones (some games limit the number of cards players can draw). The final round of betting starts after the draw with the player to the left of the dealer. There are many different and unique rules that some card rooms use and others do not. It is advisable to read the posted rules and/or ask a floor person for them before entering a Lowball game.

Ace-to-Five Lowball

A-2-3-4-5 is the best hand in Ace-to-Five Lowball. Flushes and straights do not count against you. Many Ace-to-Five Lowball games are played with a joker, which is used as the

lowest possible card. The joker, however, cannot match any card in your hand.

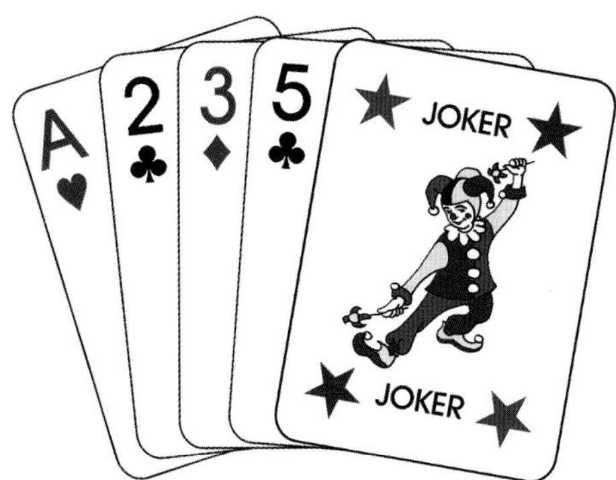

The joker represents a 4. This is the best possible hand for Ace-to-Five Lowball; it is also known as a "wheel."

Deuce-to-Seven Lowball

The best hand in Deuce-to-Seven Lowball is 2-3-4-5-7—not all of the same suit. Flushes and straights count against you. The name deuce is what many players call a two. An ace is considered only as a high card and cannot be used as a low card.

Razz

Razz is basically 7-Card Stud played for the lowest hand. All rules are the same as 7-Card Stud with the following exceptions:

- The lowest hand wins the pot. Aces are low, and flushes and straights do not count; thus the best possible hand is A-2-3-4-5.
- Unlike any hi/lo poker game, in Razz you do not have to be below a 9 to have the lowest hand; thus your highest card can be a jack, and you can still win the pot if you have the lowest hand.
- The high card showing has the forced bet after the third card is dealt, and the best low hand showing starts the betting action on all other rounds.

Good starting hands often include an ace or at least two unpaired cards five or below.

Pineapple

Pineapple is played exactly like Texas Hold'em except that each player receives three hole cards and must discard one before the flop. The betting for that round is prior to the discard.

Crazy Pineapple

Crazy Pineapple is played exactly like Texas Hold'em except that each player receives three hole cards and must discard one before the turn card is dealt. The betting for that round is also prior to the discard.

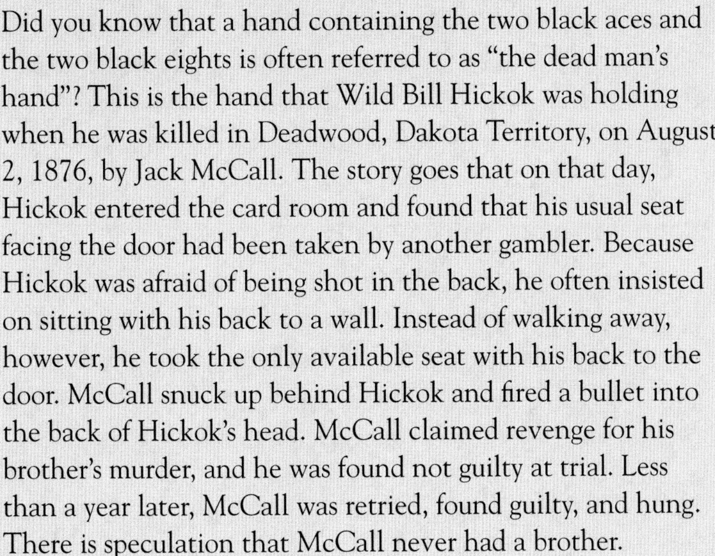

ACES AND EIGHTS: THE DEAD MAN'S HAND

Did you know that a hand containing the two black aces and the two black eights is often referred to as "the dead man's hand"? This is the hand that Wild Bill Hickok was holding when he was killed in Deadwood, Dakota Territory, on August 2, 1876, by Jack McCall. The story goes that on that day, Hickok entered the card room and found that his usual seat facing the door had been taken by another gambler. Because Hickok was afraid of being shot in the back, he often insisted on sitting with his back to a wall. Instead of walking away, however, he took the only available seat with his back to the door. McCall snuck up behind Hickok and fired a bullet into the back of Hickok's head. McCall claimed revenge for his brother's murder, and he was found not guilty at trial. Less than a year later, McCall was retried, found guilty, and hung. There is speculation that McCall never had a brother.

Chapter Six

DO THE MATH!

Every winning poker player understands the odds of winning in most situations. Though it may sound difficult at first, after reading this chapter, you will know your odds in any given situation in no time.

All poker games are games of percentages and probability. Many players play under the incorrect assumption that poker is a game of luck. In this chapter you will learn the basic percentages you will use time and time again in your poker playing. There's also a discussion on pot odds and how to use them to become a winning player. At the end of the chapter is a chart, which will be beneficial to your poker career, for it easily converts your outs (cards that can come to help you win) to pot odds for the turn, river, and both.

Poker must be viewed as one long lifetime game instead of many short sessions. The reason for this is over the course of thousands of hands, the best hand will win the correct amount of time. Poker, however, is full of short-term variance (often called luck), which can be extremely frustrating. For example: In a recent no-limit Hold'em tournament, Player A was all-in (had all of his chips in the pot) before the flop with a pair of aces against Player B who held an ace and a king. Player A's chances to win this confrontation were more than 92 percent. This means that if this situation occurs 100 times, Player A would win 92 of those times. This just happened to be one of the eight times that Player A didn't win since Player B won with trip kings. Despite losing when the odds are overwhelmingly in your favor, the goal of winning poker is still to put yourself in this type of situation as many times as possible because when you do, you will win most of the time.

Pot Odds Made Simple

Figuring pot odds is one of the most misunderstood and misused concepts for beginning poker players. In this section, simple and straightforward computations are used. And for all examples, unless otherwise noted, Texas Hold'em is the poker game being played.

Pot odds are calculations that put the concept of risk and reward into a numerical computation. For those of you who aren't confident in your math skills, don't worry. It is not complicated, and with a little practice you will be able to figure your pot odds in no time. The following examples will illustrate pot odds. We will use a 1/2 Hold'em for simplicity.

You are on the button and one of the six players in the pot for $1 each to see the flop. This makes the pot $6. You hold ♣A-♦Q, and the flop comes ♣K-♣Q-♣6.

The first player bets $1, two players call, and two players fold to bring the total in the pot to

   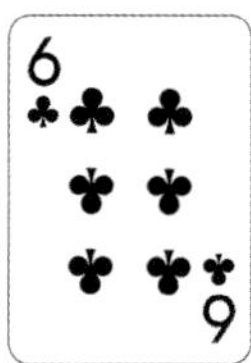

A pair of queens with a possible ace-high flush.

$9. It is now your turn to act. You must decide whether to fold, call, or raise. At this time you should assume that at least one of your opponents holds a king and that your hand must improve in order to win. Now you must decide how many unseen cards can help you win. These cards are called your "outs," and this terminology will be used from here on. (One question that is often asked is: "The other players have cards in their hands that cannot come to me on the turn or the river, so how can I count them in the cards that will improve my hand?" The answer is: You must count all cards that can help you because you have no way of knowing what cards are in your opponents' hands, even if it is quite likely that they hold certain cards. Therefore, all unseen cards need to be counted.)

Because you have a pair of queens, you must assume that if either of the other two queens hit, it will improve your hand to make you the winner. There are also three remaining aces that will improve you to two pair. This makes five outs. In addition, if any club hits, it will give you an ace high flush. So you have nine other outs (the remaining clubs). This gives you 14 outs. Now you have seen five cards (your hole cards and the three on the flop) out of a 52 card deck. This leaves 47 unseen cards before the turn. This means that 14 out of 47 cards can come on the turn and improve your hand, and 33 will not help you at all. This makes the odds roughly 2.4 to 1.

The easiest way to figure this is to see how many times your 14 outs will divide into the 33 cards that will not help you. You don't have to figure this out exactly to know if it is correct to call or not. Because 2 times 14 is 28, which is a little less than 33, and 3 times 14 equals 42, you know the number is closer to two than three. This means that for it to be correct for you to call, there must be at least 2.4 times the amount you must call in the pot. In other words, the amount you must risk, in this case $1, must have a reward of at least $2.40 when you hit your hand. In the example above, there is $9 in the pot, and you have to call only $1 to see the turn. Since the pot is offering you 9 to 1 odds, the correct play is to call or raise, which we will discuss shortly.

Pot odds boil down to percentages. The pot must be large enough to pay enough extra on the times you do hit your hand to make up for the losses when you don't. The key is to get your money into the pot when you have the best hand. If you use pot odds correctly, you will be well on your way to becoming a lifelong winner.

Continuing the above example, you call the bet on the flop, increasing the pot to $10. The turn card is ♥8, which does not improve your hand. You still have the same number of outs, 14, but one less unseen card, 46. Notice that your pot odds are almost the same, roughly 2.3 to 1. The first player bets $2, making the pot $12, and the other two players fold. The bet you must now call is $2 into a $12 dollar pot. This reduces down to 6 to 1 odds (12 divided by 2 equals 6, and 2 divided by 2 equals 1).

Once again the correct play is to call. Notice that at this time, if you don't improve on the river, you can fold, and if you do improve, you can bet or raise.

The above example is fairly simple, but what has been said is not everything you must consider. Actually, after the flop you can improve on either the turn or the river cards. This means that you have 14 outs two times, which if you consider both the turn and the river, your pot odds are actually .95 to 1. Any time your pot odds are less than 1 to 1, you are a favorite to win. In this case the correct play is often a raise instead of a call.

Some players use the combined odds for both the turn and river while others use them separately. If you use the turn odds on the turn, reevaluate the situation after the turn card is revealed, and use the pot odds on the river separately. The problem when using the combined odds is that you almost have to call on the turn to see the river even if you don't improve. This can lead to a dangerous mindset, and you can become a calling station. First, consider each situation by itself, and then, add in other factors.

More About Pot Odds

This is a good time to point out something that is often confusing to beginning players when computing pot odds. The beginning player often thinks *I already have so much money in the pot* and believes that this somehow goes into the computation of the pot odds. The fact of the matter is any money already in the pot is not yours. It was yours before you put it into the pot, and the only way you will get it back is to win the pot. This is the reason that money you have already placed into the pot is not used in computing pot odds.

Another factor to consider is something called "implied odds." Implied odds take into account not only the money in the pot and the amount of the bet but also the possibility of collecting extra bets when you hit your hand. For instance, in the above example, if all four players act before you call on the turn, more than likely one or more of them will call a bet or raise by you on the river if you hit your hand. Their calls on the river actually improve your pot odds because you can add these bets into your calculations. In this instance, you can safely figure on adding at least one and probably two bets to the pot. Be careful with your use of implied odds in close situations. It is very important not to assume future bets of which you aren't certain. Many players misread the situation and/or their opponents and rely too heavily on implied odds resulting in poor decisions. Knowing your opponents' tendencies is a must when using implied odds.

Some advanced players raise on the flop in order to give them correct pot odds to call on the turn if their hand does not improve. This is an advanced play and should be done only when you are a favorite to win the hand or have tremendous implied odds. In Chapter Seven there's a discussion of the thinking on numerous levels about what you have and what your opponents have. This is for the more advanced players who are able to think on many levels and have an excellent ability to read hands and players. If you are a novice, simply mastering your ability to understand and use pot odds should be your goal. As you

grow as a player, you will start to see situations in which you can use advanced plays such as this.

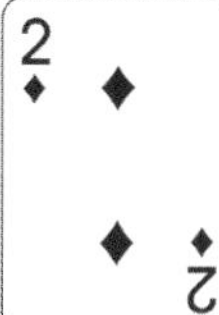

Quiz Hands

The following three quiz hands will help you get the feel of the thought process involved in using pot odds. See if you can compute the pot odds, and decide whether to call or fold. For simplicity's sake, we will not take blinds into account. (The suggested answers can be found on page 61.)

1. In a 1/2 Hold'em game, your hole cards are ♥J-♥T, and the flop is ♣K-♦Q-♥6. There

are two other players, $3 in the pot before the flop, and one player bets and the other calls. What are the odds the pot is offering you? What are the odds of improving your hand? Should you call or fold?

2. In a 1/2 Hold'em game, your hole cards are ♥J-♥T, and the flop is ♣A-♣K-♦6. There is

one other player, $2 in the pot before the flop, and your opponent bets $1. What are the odds the pot is offering you? What are the odds of improving your hand? Should you call or fold?

3. In a 1/2 Hold'em game, your hole cards are ♦Q-♥Q, the flop is ♦2-♥T-♠7, and the turn is ♣A. You are the last to act and must call a $2 bet to see the river. There is $34 in the pot. What are the odds the pot is offering you? What are the odds of improving your hand? Should you call or fold?

These examples are fairly simple, and hopefully you can see how pot odds can work for you. Once you have a good understanding, use the chart on the next page and practice. Pot odds are the only difference between some winning and losing players—they are that important. So learn to compute them or memorize the chart, but make the commitment to use pot odds when playing poker. You'll never regret it, and neither will your bankroll.

Many poker players talk about EV, which stands for "Expected Value." Expected value is the amount you can expect to win on average every time you are in a particular situation. It

MONEYMAKER THE MONEYMAKER

The 2003 World Series of Poker main event champion was an amateur poker player and accountant named Chris Moneymaker. Talk about a prophetic last name! Moneymaker earned his seat in the World Series main event by winning an on-line satellite tournament with a $39 buy-in. The first-place prize he collected at the World Series of Poker was $2.5 million! What a return on investment. More than 800 players entered the main event, setting the record at that time.

POT ODDS				
Number of Outs	**Turn**	**River**	**Turn & River Combined**	**Example**
1	46-1	45-1	22.3-1	
2	22.5-1	22-1	10.9-1	
3	14.7-1	14.3-1	7-1	
4	10.8-1	10.5-1	5.1-1	Gutshot Straight
5	8.4-1	8.2-1	3.9-1	
6	6.8-1	6.7-1	3.2-1	
7	5.7-1	5.6-1	2.6-1	
8	4.9-1	4.8-1	2.2-1	Open End Straight
9	4.2-1	4.1-1	1.9-1	Flush
10	3.7-1	3.6-1	1.6-1	
11	3.3-1	3.2-1	1.4-1	
12	2.9-1	2.8-1	1.2-1	
13	2.6-1	2.5-1	1.1-1	
14	2.4-1	2.3-1	.95-1	
15	2.1-1	2.1-1	.85-1	Flush & Straight
16	1.9-1	1.9-1	.75-1	
17	1.8-1	1.7-1	.67-1	
18	1.6-1	1.6-1	.60-1	
19	1.5-1	1.4-1	.54-1	
20	1.3-1	1.3-1	.48-1	

is included here because as you spend more time playing poker, you will hear EV tossed around, and you should know what it is.

Using an earlier example in this chapter, assume you have a pair of aces, and you place a $100 bet and one player calls with AK. The way to determine your EV is as follows: Put yourself in this situation 100 times. (It costs you $10,000 [$100 times 100] to enter this situation 100 times.) You will win 92 times and receive your $100 in return plus your opponent's $100 for a total of $18,400. You will lose your $100 the other eight times. Therefore, your $10,000 nets you $8,400 in profit ($18,400 minus $10,000). Now divide the profit ($8,400) by 100 times, and this figure—$84—equals your EV. What this tells you is that, on average, you will win $84 every time you are in this same situation. Good poker players maximize the times they have positive EV and minimize the times they have negative EV.

Chapter Seven

PSYCHING YOUR OPPONENTS

Become a winning poker player by minimizing your tilts, recognizing tells, learning to read situations and opponents, and thinking on many levels.

Any long-time poker player will tell you that to be a good player you must think about many different things while you are playing. In this chapter, four important psychological concepts will be discussed: tilts, tells, reading hands and situations, and thinking on many levels.

Tilts

When players make mistakes because something upsets them emotionally, it is called a "tilt" or "being on a tilt." An example is a player who is a huge favorite in a hand but loses to an opponent who hits a miracle card on the river (often called a "bad beat"). That player becomes so emotionally upset that he/she begins to make bad decisions. Another instance that sometimes puts players on a tilt is when an opponent is loud, obnoxious, rude, or otherwise annoying. Players who are on a tilt react in many different ways with the most common being entering pots with weaker hands than usual and calling bets when the pot odds don't warrant it. While it's important to realize when one of your opponents is on a tilt, it is more important to realize when *you* may be going on a tilt and figuring out how not to let your emotions get the best of you.

Recognizing when you are going on a tilt is easier for some than others. If you think you may have played on tilt but aren't sure, one way that may help you is to keep detailed records of your playing sessions. Something else to watch out for is if you start to consider playing weaker hands than you usually play after taking a couple bad beats.

Once you realize that you are going on a tilt, you must, of course, try to avoid it. Some players can avoid tilting by simply suppressing their emotions and concentrating more on the game. If you are too upset, it may be best to simply quit your current playing session. Some players will get up and take a short walk to clear their head before returning to the game. Some find that fresh air also helps. Try different things when you go on a tilt until you find which one works best for you.

When one of your opponents is on a tilt, remember a few things as you try to take advantage of the situation. Players on a tilt are often unpredictable, especially when deciding their starting hand. Entering the pot with weaker hands than usual is the most common thing players on a tilt do. Another thing to remember is that players may realize what they

are doing and correct it at any time. In addition, solid players may be trying to convince you they are on a tilt when they are not. Deception in poker is a frequent occurrence. It is important to remember not to play weak hands in order to take advantage of the player on a tilt. The fish may become so tempting to you that you become a fish yourself.

Tells

When players act in a way that gives away something about their hand, it is called a "tell." Much like a tilt, it is important not only to recognize your opponents' tells but also to realize if you have any.

Some players' hands shake when they are placing a bet if they have a very strong hand, while other players' hands shake when they are bluffing. Some players act strong when they are weak and act weak when they are strong. These players will often bet aggressively by practically throwing their chips into the pot or even toward you in hopes that their show of strength will make you fold.

Players who have a large pocket pair in Hold'em—like AA or KK—will sometimes closely watch each other place their bet into the pot as if making sure that nobody shorts the pot. These players have already won the hand in their mind and want to make sure that they collect every last bet. And then there are some players who hold their breath when they have a strong hand.

There is an unlimited number of possible tells, for it is human nature to react in some way when excited, and everyone is different. Picking up tells on your opponents can be done only by paying attention to detail. So practice concentrating on your opponents as much as possible while hiding any tells you may have. Learning to control your emotions under many situations takes practice, but it is very important because poker is a game of information, and you don't want to give any more of it away than you have to. If you are able to, your game will certainly improve.

Reading Hands and Situations

Reading hands and situations is a skill that can be mastered only by practice and experience. Over time, you can read many players because they fall into patterns and become predictable. For instance, some players raise before the flop only with strong hands like AA, KK, and AK.

Don't always raise with these very strong starters.

These players reveal too much information about their playing styles to their opponents by always playing this way.

What you must constantly look for is betting patterns. Many players bet the same type of hands the same way every time. If you can pick up on their patterns, it will improve your game tremendously. Many players, when on a draw, will call bets on the flop and turn. Then, they will always raise on the river when they hit their hand, and check or fold when they don't. One lesson to be learned from this tendency is to occasionally vary your own play so an opponent can't easily read your hands.

T.J. CLOUTIER

T. J. Cloutier is probably today's best tournament poker player. He has won more than 50 tournaments with buy-ins of $500 or more. This gentle giant played tight end in the Canadian Football League for five years. Though he has never won the main event at the World Series of Poker, he was the first player to win more than $1 million without winning the title. At the poker table, he is respected by many professional poker players and feared by the rest. From his vast experience and powers of observation, he is one of the best in the game in his ability to read players and situations and pick up tells.

Usually making a play that is contrary to your normal playing style is only necessary about 5 percent of the time to keep your opponents guessing. This, however, is only necessary in a game with opponents who are paying attention. Poor players rarely notice anything you do out of the ordinary, so just play simple straightforward poker against them.

As you become more experienced, you will learn to read situations and know what is going to happen. A common example of this is when you have a top pair and a good kicker or two pair on the flop, which contains two cards of the same suit. You bet on the flop and are called. You bet again on the turn and are called. Then on the river the third card of a suit hits making a flush possible. After you bet again, the person who had been calling raises you. In low-limit Hold'em, this means a flush will beat you almost every time. The only time you may not be beaten is when a solid player feels that you are capable of laying down a good hand for one bet and is bluffing you because of the scare card. This is often not the case. Situations such as this are learned with experience. So practice, practice, practice.

Another reason it is important to pay close attention to the game is so you will think back about how a hand has been played to the present. Did anyone raise before the flop? If so, who raised? Has someone who has been checking and calling suddenly raised? You need to answer these questions in order to recognize and read situations at the poker table.

Thinking on Many Levels

One of the biggest advantages that most professional players have over amateurs is the ability to think on many levels. This means thinking about what you have, what your opponent has, what your opponent thinks you have, and so on.

Thinking beyond the first two or three levels is rarely necessary in low-limit Hold'em, but as you advance in limits, it becomes necessary to think on many levels. Remember that poker is a game of information, and the better your opponents play, the more information you will need to be successful.

QUESTIONS

1. What is a tilt?
2. How often should you raise with this hand?

3. What are levels, and why are they important?

(Answers are on pages 61–62.)

Chapter Eight

CASINO POINTERS AND ETIQUETTE

Read this chapter to find some helpful advice on your first trip to a casino or poker room, including some do's and don'ts.

If you have never been to a casino or public poker room before, your first trip can be filled with excitement, anticipation, and exhilaration. It may also cause you a little fear and apprehension. This chapter gives you a few pointers and some information about how things work in most casinos and public poker rooms. Always remember that everyone who is a regular in the card room was once new, too.

The Staff

A great way to make your first trip less stressful is to go with a friend who has been there before. But if this option is not available, don't let that stop you. One of the most important things to remember is that the staff of a casino or poker room is there to make your visit as comfortable as possible because they want you to come back. If you can't find the card room or if you have any questions at all, don't hesitate to ask a staff member.

The dealer is also part of the staff. If you are sitting down at a poker game in a casino or card room for the first time, tell the dealer that it is your first time and ask them to please keep an eye on you to make sure you aren't doing anything incorrectly. You may be amazed at how helpful and useful someone can be when you show them a little respect and ask for their help. Many times, especially at the lower-limit tables, other players are also helpful.

Waiting List and Chips

Most poker rooms have a place to sign a waiting list for a particular game. Some have a white board with the games and limits avail-

> **THE WORLD SERIES OF POKER**
>
> The World Series of Poker is the most important poker event in the world. It has been held every year since 1970. The 2004 event had a record number of entrants (more than 2,500) and the winner of the $10,000 buy-in main event Texas Hold'em championship was Greg Raymer, who won $5 million. Raymer is nicknamed "Fossilman" because he uses a small fossil to protect his cards at the table. He was the second winner of the main event in as many years to win his seat in the tournament through an online qualifying tournament. Many Internet poker sites have online tournaments in which the winners receive a free seat at the main event at the World Series of Poker.

able along with the waiting players' initials. Others will just have someone who writes initials or names on a sheet of paper. The card room calls the next person on the list when a seat becomes available. Simply ask whoever is in charge of the board—or a staff member—to place you on the list for all of the games you are willing to play. If you are in a small poker room with no visible sign-up area, ask a dealer how to enter a game.

Useful Tips

Here are some tips for your first game:

1. Wait for the big blind to get to you before playing. Use this time to watch your opponents, and get a feel for the way they are playing. It's amazing how many tells some players have if you just pay attention.

2. Most players tip the dealer when they win a pot. This is not required, but if the dealer is doing a competent job, you should tip. Dealers are like waitstaff in that they make most of their money from tips. A sample plan would be to tip the dealer .50 on average size pots and possibly $1.00 on larger pots if the dealer is doing a good job. Also, you can watch what the other players are tipping to get an idea. Remember though that every dollar that goes to the dealer is reducing your winnings. You should be able to come to a happy medium with experience.

3. Act when it's your turn. Never act before your turn. This is very poor etiquette and can change the outcome of a hand. The other players will understandably get upset with you.

4. Make sure your cards are in plain sight. It is a good idea to place a chip on them to show that they are still live and protect them because the dealer won't take them when the chip is on them. If you leave your hole cards unprotected, the dealer might muck them (mix with discards) by mistake, and there is no way you can retrieve them. Most players keep their hand on their cards.

5. When you win a pot, don't reach for it. Let the dealer push the pot to you. Do not surrender your cards until the pot has been awarded to you on a winning hand.

6. If you aren't sure whether you have the best hand at the end of a round, turn your cards face up, and let the dealer read the hands. If the dealer makes a mistake, it can often be corrected. If you throw your hand into the discard pile (often called the "muck"), you are not eligible for any of the pot even if you made a mistake and had the best hand.

7. Don't make a string-bet. A string-bet is calling a bet and then raising it at the same turn. The best way to avoid this error is to state what you are doing. If you plan to call, simply say, "I call." If you plan to raise, say, "I raise." By announcing your intentions, there won't be any question. If a dealer doesn't catch a string-bet, usually another player will, and the string-bet will be disallowed.

8. Don't throw your chips into the pot (called "splashing" the pot). Place all bets in front of you, and let the dealer pull them into the pot.

Chapter Nine
TOURNAMENT PLAY

Whether you are an experienced tournament player or just starting, you have turned to the right chapter to improve your chance at tournament success.

Tournament poker, especially no-limit Hold'em, has been growing in popularity at tremendous rates over the past few years. As discussed in the introduction, television coverage has had a great impact on poker. What you see on television most of the time is the final table of a large poker tournament. Most tournaments follow the same basic structure.

Player's Choice

Always find out the exact structure that a tournament will use before you enter, including the game, limit, blind structure, ante structure, pay-out percentage, and places paid.

Here is an example of a no-limit Hold'em tournament structure based on 100 entrants, each paying $110. (One hundred dollars goes to the prize pool and the other $10 is the entry fee, making the total prize pool $10,000.) The top ten places pay the following percentage of the prize pool. (Most tournaments pay out to the top 10 percent.)

1.	$4,000	(40%)	**6.**	$500	(5%)
2.	$2,000	(20%)	**7.**	$400	(4%)
3.	$1,000	(10%)	**8.**	$300	(3%)
4.	$800	(8%)	**9.**	$200	(2%)
5.	$650	(6.5%)	**10.**	$150	(1.5%)

Everyone starts with 1,000 in tournament chips, and the blinds start at 10/20 and raise every hour (called levels), using the following schedule:

Level	Blinds	Ante
1	10/20	0
2	20/40	0
3	40/80	0
4	50/100	20
5	100/200	50
6	200/400	100
7	300/600	150
8	500/1,000	200
9	1,000/2,000	500
10	2,500/5,000	1,000

Notice that the blinds increase every hour and quickly reach a point that forces players with smaller amounts of chips (stacks) to take chances to keep from having the blinds eliminate them. Most tournaments are set up along this line in order to force action and to have a good idea of when the tournament will end.

Knowing how fast the blinds raise is an important element to consider before entering a tournament since the slower the blinds raise, the more the outcome will depend on a player's skill than on luck. Another important

consideration is how many places pay and how much they pay. Some tournaments are top heavy, paying the largest amount of money to the top few finishers while other tournaments spread out the prize money more evenly—sometimes paying out to the top 20 percent of entrants.

Some tournaments offer an opportunity to rebuy, usually within a set time limit if you lose all of your chips. We will discuss the part of the tournament after the rebuy period or a tournament that doesn't offer a rebuy option.

Tournament Strategy

The biggest difference between a tournament and a normal ring game is that once your chips are gone in a tournament, you are out of the tournament. In a regular ring game, you have the option to buy more chips at any time between hands. This makes tournament strategy a little different. Some players simply want to place in the money while others play to win. The obvious question is why doesn't everyone play to win? The answer has to do with the variance associated with two different playing styles.

Many players who are playing to win will move all their chips in with even the slightest advantage, sometimes as low as a 52- or 53-percent chance to win any given hand. If cards break their way, they can accumulate a large stack of chips, which is needed to win late in the tournament. Getting all of your chips into the pot, however, in marginal situations such as these often leads to busting out of a tournament early when cards don't go your way.

Players who just want to get into the money usually play much tighter, trying to get better odds (often as high as 80 or 85 percent) before they push their chips into the pot. The problem with this approach is that the blinds usually eat a large part of their stack between these opportunities.

The correct strategy to become a successful tournament player is somewhere in between these two styles. As always, you should bet when you are a favorite to win, but in close situations in a tournament it may be best to hold back unless you are getting short stacked. If your stack gets too low, you will be forced to choose a good starting hand and probably bet all of your chips, hoping no one else has a better hand.

In the early stages of a tournament before the blinds get too high, playing very tight is recommended; that is, only entering the pot with your best hands. If the opportunity to get all of your

THE WORLD POKER TOUR

The *World Poker Tour* is a collection of televised tournaments. In fact, it was the first nationally available, regularly scheduled poker program on TV. The *World Poker Tour* has made Wednesday nights poker night in many homes and is partly responsible for the recent poker boom. Developed and created by Lyle Berman and hosted by Mike Sexton, the ratings have been steadily climbing from the first episode. During the first year, the reruns were drawing more viewers than the originals. The *World Poker Tour* has become so popular that you can even buy stock in it. Check the symbol WPTE on the NASDAQ.

money in with at least one other person while you have AA, KK, or maybe QQ, then by all means take it. If you are able to double-up early in a tournament, it not only gives you extra chips, but it also can be a tremendous psychological advantage by having a large stack. As you go deeper into the tournament, the larger the stack you have, the more you can force your opponents with fewer chips to lay down their hands instead of risking all of their chips against you.

Most tournaments are no-limit Hold'em, which brings up the need to discuss a few important points. Making just one mistake can end your tournament because all of your chips can end up in the pot at any time. For this reason it is important to play to the best of your abilities at all times. You must learn as much about your opponents' play as possible. Always pay attention, and do your best not to lose concentration for even a second.

The next important point involves pot odds. As mentioned in the advanced Hold'em section, no-limit Hold'em allows you to make the perfect size bet to cause the pot odds to be unfavorable to an opponent. It is important to realize which opponents will use pot odds and which will not, because trying to make an opponent (who does not recognize pot odds) fold can be a risky proposition. On the other hand, you can make the pot odds favorable to the players who use pot odds by placing a bet of a particular amount in order to induce a call.

Tournament play has many similarities to ring game play, but it also has many differences. Complete books are dedicated to tournament play, and there isn't enough room in this book to explore the finer points. If you use the information contained in this chapter along with your experience, however, you can become a good tournament player.

There is one last important point that you should be aware of. Though it may appear differently because of the television coverage of tournaments, very few professional players make their living playing tournament poker. Most professional poker players earn their living playing in ring games. Because of the accelerated blind structures, tournaments often require a few lucky breaks in order to win. This often works against the professional players who know how to make correct plays. A perfect example of this was the 2004 World Series of Poker final. The professional players as a whole didn't fair well because amateur and recreational players greatly outnumbered them. In the long run, if the professionals played against the players in this field, they would eventually win most, if not all, of the money. But because of the tournament structure, they didn't have the necessary time to do it. Professional players don't depend on luck, just mathematical facts.

QUESTIONS

1. What is the biggest difference between tournament play and ring game play?
2. Why must you play to the best of your abilities at all times in no-limit tournament play?
3. Why are pot odds a good player's best friend in a no-limit tournament?

(Answers are on page 62.)

Chapter Ten

CYBERSPACE POKER

Hundreds of thousands of people play poker on the Internet every day. Find information, tips, and strategies here to start your voyage into cyberspace.

Hand-in-hand with television in the recent surge in popularity of poker is the opportunity to play poker on the Internet. You can find an online poker game any time of the day or night. You can play for free or for real money against players from all over the world. There are thousands of ring games at virtually any level as well as thousands of tournaments ranging in size from ten entrants up to thousands with buy-ins ranging from free up to thousands of dollars. The following games, and others, are readily available online.

Popular Internet Poker Games

Texas Hold'em
Limit
Pot-limit
No-limit

Omaha/8
Limit
Pot-limit

Omaha High
Limit
Pot-limit

Seven-Card Stud
Limit
Pot-limit

Pineapple

Razz

Five-Card Draw

Triple Draw

The Benefits of Internet Play

Playing poker on the Internet is a tremendous way to gain experience and also less expensive than traveling to a card room. Most players tip the dealer when they win a hand in a brick-and-mortar card room (often called B&M) and also often tip the servers when they bring a drink or food. Playing on the Internet requires no tipping. Thus these expenses, as well as the travel expenses associated with live play are nonexistent. In addition, you play many more hands per hour online because a dealer doesn't have to take the time to shuffle, and the play is faster because most online poker sites have a time limit for each player to act.

Exactly like their live counterparts, online poker sites make money from collecting a rake from each pot in limit games or an entry fee for tournaments. Rake is a percentage of each pot the house keeps, which is often 5 percent with a cap depending on the limit of the game. It is advisable to find out how much the rake is

before playing in games either online or in a B&M card room.

Internet-based poker rooms are fairly new in comparison to B&M rooms. The first ones were available in the late 1990s and were slow due to many technical difficulties. Like all technology, however, online poker rooms quickly improved, and currently they are fast, efficient, pleasant looking, and technically sound.

Right now there are more than 200 Internet poker rooms. The largest Internet poker room has over 50,000 people playing at the same time during peak playing hours. Just do an Internet search for poker or take a look at some of the online poker-related sites, and you will quickly find many places to play and thousands upon thousands of pages of information.

Many sites use the same software, and players from these sites play in the same virtual room. These are called "networks," and each individual site is called a "skin." Often you can have an account and play at more than one site on a network. The reason you may want to do this is because most sites have bonus offers. (These are discussed in the next section.) These networks are necessary to populate a poker room to offer a fair selection of games and limits. There are ten of these networks that have 2,500 or more players at peak times. Thus your online options are plentiful. Because the largest sites have full games at every level at any time of day, there is always a place to play.

Bonus Offers

The online poker business is highly competitive. As mentioned above, poker rooms make money from players in the form of rakes and entry fees. The more players a site has, the more revenue it will generate. For this reason, it seems as though every site has bonus offers to attract new players. Practically every site offers a bonus on a player's first deposit ranging from 20 percent (deposit $100 and receive a $20 bonus) up to 100 percent (deposit $100 and get a $100 bonus). These deposit bonuses are usually tied to a requirement to play a pre determined amount of raked hands (a raked hand is one game in which money has been contributed to a pot and the house has taken a small percentage from the pot). Before depositing in any online site, make sure you have read the terms and conditions so you know exactly what you must do to receive the bonus.

Many sites also periodically offer reload bonuses (usually requiring another deposit under the same terms and conditions as a first-

SEARCHING THE WEB FOR POKER

Just type in the word "poker" in any Internet search engine, and you'll find millions of listings! You can find sites to play poker, read about the history of poker, learn about the best players, and discover strategies and recommendations for every imaginable poker game. In addition, there are many forums to discuss your experiences and ask for advice from players around the world. The Internet can be a tremendous learning tool for anyone wanting to improve their game. Just find those sites that most interest you, and read away.

time bonus) to current players to entice them to keep playing at the site. Many players continuously move from site to site collecting these bonuses (often called bonus hunting), which can be a good way to increase a player's profit per hour of poker play. In addition, if you are able to simply play break-even poker, bonuses can make you a profit as you improve your game.

Internet Regulations

Playing poker on the Internet is not for everyone. Because all Internet poker rooms are based outside of the United States, the laws and regulations governing them are different from what many players are familiar with. For this reason, it is recommended playing at only the larger, well-established sites when you first start playing online—and only if it is legal!

Because many sites do not accept credit cards, you must set up a virtual bank account of some kind to fund your poker account. When doing this, choose one that has been in business for a while and has many customers. A deposit into a poker site is put into your account. Money you lose is deducted from your account, and money you win is put into your account.

Learn on the Web

For players who are just learning to play poker or are learning a new game they have little or no experience with, online poker offers a wonderful arena to increase skill, knowledge of the game, and possibly build a bankroll at the same time. Most sites offer the opportunity to play poker for free, using play money. Some sites even have "free rolls," which are tournaments you may enter for free that pay out real money to the winners. In addition, many sites offer real money limits as low as .01/.02. The largest entry level limit at any site currently is 1/2.

The play at the free money tables is not very good, and it is recommended using them only to get a feel for the gaming software and/or to learn a new game. The smaller games of .01/.02 up to .25/.50 (often called micro limits) offer a slightly more realistic feel to a poker game because you play for real money, but the play is horrendous. As you climb in levels, the play improves, but some games as high as 3/6 and 5/10 can have some inexperienced players, just like at a live poker room.

Plan of Action

A quick way to start playing poker on the Internet is to set aside a small amount of money ($20 to $100) as a test bankroll. Open an Internet bank account (search the Internet for e-payment systems), and then find a couple of established online poker rooms that offer the opportunity to play for free, afford micro-limit games, and provide a sign-up bonus. Download the software and play the free games until you have a good feel for how it works. Then deposit your money, and start playing the micro-limit tables.

Use 300 times the big bet guidelines (which is discussed in Chapter Eleven) to decide at what limit to start. For example, if you want to play .25/.50, start with a bankroll of $150. Then, don't move up in limits until you have won enough to cover 300 times the big bet for the next level. Of course, it is never recommended playing at a level higher than you are comfortable with, no matter how small the

stakes. This way you will be gaining valuable experience while improving your game and hopefully building your bankroll.

Many players jump right into a game that has higher limits before they are ready for it, and then they lose a lot of money before dropping back down in limits. Use these guidelines, and don't move up until you are ready. There is no shame in playing poker for pennies. If you do move up to a higher level and struggle, don't hesitate to move back down. Because poker is a lifelong game, players must never stop learning, and the Internet is just another study aid.

(Any and all material in this chapter is for informational purposes only. Nothing in this chapter is intended as, nor should be perceived as, legal advice. Before playing poker on the Internet for real money, check your local, state, and national laws to determine the laws that govern your area.)

QUESTIONS

1. When did the first Internet-based poker rooms become available?
2. How do Internet poker sites make money?
3. What is the number-one reason for not playing poker on the web in your particular area?

(Answers are on page 62.)

Chapter Eleven

ACCOUNTING 101—YOUR BANKROLL

Find out how much money you need to play poker at any limit, and learn one last thing that separates good players from bad.

A bankroll is the amount of money you have available to play poker. Nevertheless, the most important thing you should know about money management while playing poker is that until you become a consistent winner, it doesn't matter how big your bankroll is; the only thing that matters is how much you have to lose. With this in mind, the information contained in this chapter is a guideline for your bankroll once you have become a winning player.

Bankroll vs. Buy-in

Some beginning players confuse the terms "bankroll" and "buy-in." A buy-in is the amount of money you start with in a game or the entry fee into a tournament. Your bankroll is the entire amount of money you have available with which to play poker over a period of time. Keep in mind that at a casino or poker room you may have money in reserve to buy chips if your stake becomes too low or if you are afforded the opportunity to rebuy in a tournament. For example, you may have a bankroll of $2,000, and you play 5/10 limit Hold'em. If this is the case, you would probably buy in for $200 in a ring game and have $200 in reserve. It would be unwise to bring your entire bankroll at any one time or to use all the money you have with you to buy chips right off. Not only are there ups-and-downs during a single poker session but also ups-and-downs over a period of time. Your bankroll should tide you over the low periods. If not, then you need to think about how poker is affecting your overall finances.

One more point about digging into your reserve when your chip stack is low. In a ring game, it is never advisable to wait until your stack is depleted before buying more chips. If your stack is too low, you can't play with strength, and you are often on a tilt. It is better to buy more "ammo" (chips) before your stack gets low or end this particular playing session. It is not so much that you walk away from the poker table with something, it is that you won't play those chips from a position of weakness, which rarely wins. To be able to walk away in this situation takes discipline, which marks the good players from the bad players.

Bankroll Recommendations

Bankroll-size suggestions range from 200 times the big bet at the level you are playing (for example, $400 at 1/2) to 300 times the big bet ($600 at 1/2). These amounts may seem like

large numbers, but the fact is that even consistent winning professional poker players have downswings in their bankroll that may sometimes reach 200 times the big bet of the limits at which they are playing. Any number of factors or a combination of factors may cause these downswings. They include a run of bad cards, poor play for one reason or another, poor game or table selection, or health issues.

It is recommended to start with 300 times the big bet. A lot of players play much better when they have this cushion. Some have played at levels in which they had less than 100 times the big bet in their bankroll, and it usually hurts their play. This is obviously a purely psychological hurdle, but when reduced to facts, it makes sense. Keep in mind that 50 times the big bet is a fairly common downswing and nothing to become too concerned about if you are still playing to the best of your ability.

If, however, you start with only 100 times the big bet and are down 50 big bets, you have lost 50 percent of your bankroll. If you had started with 300 big bets and are down 50, you have only lost roughly 17 percent of your bankroll. This is a huge difference because many players who lose a large amount of their bankroll will start pressing and make poor decisions, which compounds the problem.

This advice is not to say that you should never take a shot at the next level. For example, you have been playing 5/10 Hold'em fairly successfully on a bankroll of $3,000. You walk into your favorite card room and find the 5/10 game full with a long waiting list, but there is an open seat at the 10/20 table. In addition, you see three players that you have played against many times before who are not very good poker players in the 10/20 game. This may be a perfect time to take a shot at that next level. Notice that this situation is nearly perfect. It is assumed that you are well rested and fresh because you are just getting to the card room, you have been playing well, and the game selection looks good. Even with all of these factors in your favor, however, you must be able to psychologically handle this higher level and be able to drop back to your normal limits if things don't go well instead of trying to get even. Trying to just break-even when you are down is a thought that should never enter your mind.

An Accurate Poker Record

One last suggestion that is extremely important on your trip to becoming a successful

SUGGESTED RECORD OF POKER PLAYING

1.	Date of playing session	(2/2/05)
2.	Time started playing session	(8:02 P.M.)
3.	Time finished playing session	(11:30 P.M.)
4.	Buy in	($100)
5.	Cash out	($112)
6.	Location of playing session	(Uncle Bob's)
7.	Game	(Hold'em)
8.	Limit	(2/4)
9.	Notes	(New player Bill, the Aggressive Player)

Examples are in parenthesis.

poker player is record keeping. If you take nothing else from this entire book, follow this advice: Keep Accurate Records. This bit of advice is very important. Keeping accurate records is the only way you will be able to make logical and educated decisions for your poker career. Some players keep very extensive records while others keep none at all. It is recommended keeping track of at least the data contained in the sidebar "Suggested Record of Poker Playing."

By keeping these records you will be able to tell over time if there are any trends you need to be aware of and also just how profitable your poker playing is. You will be able to compare your winnings (usually measured in wins per hour) in different games, at different limits, at different times, and at different locations. For example: Solid players usually average 1 to 1.5 wins per hour.

Remember, poker is a game of information. This is just one more weapon on the road to playing poker like a pro.

QUESTIONS

1. What is a bankroll?
2. What size bankroll should you have in comparison to the big bet of the level you are playing?
3. According to this chapter, what is this book's most important suggestion?

(Answers are on page 62.)

ANSWERS

Chapter Two

1. A pair of aces.

2. Your opponents are usually better and tighter players.

3. AA, KK, and AK.

4. You should not call. You should either fold or raise, depending on how good you are at reading the other players and playing after the flop. In a game of good players, the problem with entering the pot with your tens is you are probably beat if any ace or king hits, and you must bluff successfully to win the pot. Moreover, because good players may see the flop with A-Q or even A-Js in this situation, any card over a ten is probably bad for you. Also, what do you do if one of your opponents reraises you before the flop? The answer is fold, as you are dominated. Most poor players who raise with this type of hand don't understand that being reraised before the flop is actually good, for it provides them with important information by letting them know exactly where they stand. At this point you may decide to call the raise because of pot odds. Then, if you don't improve on the flop and if there is additional betting, you should fold.

5. Raise. Your goal should be to play heads-up with the raiser, who can be stronger only with a pair of aces. By placing the second raise, it forces the blinds to fold unless they have strong hands. Remember, the more players who see the flop, the less likely your kings will win.

Chapter Three

1. A, A, 2, 3 with both aces suited. For example ♠A-♥A-♠2-♥3. With these cards you have a chance to scoop the pot with both high and low. For high, you have a chance at an ace-high flush in two suits, a straight, and even aces full. Meanwhile, you have the three lowest cards, and if a community card counterfeits your ace, you have at least trip aces and still the 2 and 3 for the best low.

2. Let's look at two hands, one with A, 2, 3, 5 and one with A, 2, Q, K. If the flop comes 4, 6, 7 you have the best possible low hand with both hands. If, however, an A or 2 falls on the turn or river, the hand with A, 2, Q, K no longer has the best possible low while the other hand still does. This is called counterfeit protection and is very important to a winning Omaha/8 strategy.

3. Flush draws with low-suited cards are far more important in Omaha/8 because they can scoop the pot. If there is a low, the low hole cards could take low, and if the flush hits, it could take high. In Hold'em, because it is harder to make a flush with fewer hole cards, and the chance of winning with low cards is far less, good players will discard low-suited hole cards.

Chapter Four

1. AAA.

2. Memory. It is important to remember what cards your opponents had before folding

to determine what cards remain in the deck to improve your hand. In Hold'em and Omaha, you never see your opponents' cards.

3. Usually you should fold because you know you are beat. Of course, you can bluff, trying to con your opponent into thinking you have aces full, which would beat any full house your opponent may have.

Chapter Six

1. The odds the pot is offering you are 5 to 1. There is $5 in the pot, and you need to call with $1. Because any ace or nine will give you a straight, you have 8 outs of the 47 unseen cards or almost 4.9 to 1 odds to improve your hand. In a loose game where you can expect one or both of your opponents to pay you off when you hit, you should call. In a tight game with solid opponents, this is probably a fold. If you do decide to see the turn and another heart hits, your outs go from 8 to 17, and the pot odds probably improve enough to see the river.

Some may wonder why the possibility of a straight with a heart flush isn't an automatic call on the flop. While it's true that the possibility of two hearts hitting the turn and river (often called runner-runner) improve your odds slightly, the odds are knocked back down by the fact that if you hit a flush, it may not be the best flush because the ♥A is out and may be in an opponent's hand; or if you improve to two pair, you could be beat by trips. Remember, don't ever let the possibility of runner-runner enter into your calculations until the first runner hits. When you need two cards to make a hand (often called a two-outer), you are getting terrible odds.

2. The odds the pot is offering you are 3 to 1. In all likelihood, your opponent holds an ace or a king, so making a pair will not help. Your only hope is making a straight. Therefore, you have only 4 outs (the 4 queens). This makes the odds 10.8 to 1 that you will hit your hand. This is an easy fold.

3. The odds the pot is offering you are 17 to 1. You are definitely up against at least a pair of aces and probably trips. You must have a queen on the river to win (unless your opponent has trip aces in which case you cannot win). This leaves you with 2 outs to win the hand and makes the odds 22 to 1. Though this looks like a fold, it is recommended calling in this situation despite the possibility of pocket aces because of the implied odds. Your hand is well disguised, and if a queen hits, none of your opponents will put you on trips, so you should be able to collect at least two or three more bets and possibly more since one of your opponents will almost definitely bet into you and you can raise.

Chapter Seven

1. A player is on a "tilt" when they are emotionally upset and start making poor poker decisions. It can be caused by a losing hand or an obnoxious opponent.

2. About 95% of the time.

3. Levels means thinking about what you have, what your opponent has, what your opponent thinks you have, what your opponent thinks you think he/she has, and so on. Thinking beyond the first two or three levels is rarely necessary in low-limit Hold'em, but as

you advance in limits and as your opponents become stronger players, it becomes necessary to think on many levels. Remember that poker is a game of information, and the better your opponents play, the more information you will need to be successful.

Chapter Nine

1. The biggest difference between tournament play and ring game play is that once your chips are gone, you are out of the tournament (unless it allows for early rebuys, but even those that do will not allow rebuys toward the end of tournament play). In a regular ring game you have the option to buy more chips at any time.

2. Making just one mistake can end your tournament because all of your chips can end up in the pot at any time.

3. As mentioned in the advanced Hold'em section, no-limit Hold'em allows you to make the perfect-size bet to cause the pot odds to be unfavorable to your opponent.

Chapter Ten

1. The first Internet-based poker rooms became available in the late 1990s.

2. Exactly like their live counterparts (B&M card rooms), online poker sites make money from collecting a rake from each pot in limit games or an entry fee for tournaments.

3. If it is illegal.

Chapter Eleven

1. A bankroll is the amount of money you have available to play poker with over a particular period of time. For example, your bankroll may be $1,000 over a year.

2. If at all possible, start with 300 times the big bet.

3. Keep records, and keep them accurately.

GLOSSARY

Action: The betting within a poker hand. If you bet first, you are starting the action. Games described as having a lot of action have a lot of betting.

All-In: To place all of the chips you have on the table into the pot.

Back Door: A draw that requires two cards to complete a straight, flush, or full house. For example, to complete a flush the correct suit must hit on the turn *and* the river.

Bad Beat: Losing a hand in which you were a decisive favorite to win before the river card.

Bankroll: The amount of money you have available with which to play poker over a particular period of time.

Best of It: To be a favorite to win.

Bet: To place money into the pot.

Blind: Forced bet that must be made before the cards are dealt.

Bluff: To bet with an inferior hand in the hope that your opponents will fold.

Board: Community cards.

Bottom Pair: Having a pair containing the lowest card on the board.

Button: A token that represents the dealer position (the last to act in most games after the first round).

Call: To place an amount of money equal to a previous opponent's bet.

Check: To decline to bet or to pass when it is your turn to act.

Check-Raise: To check and then raise if an opponent bets.

Community Cards: Cards placed in the middle of the table and shared by all players.

Drawing Dead: Drawing to a hand that, even if it hits, will lose to a hand that is already better.

Expected Value (EV): The average amount you will win when betting in the same situation numerous times.

Favorite: To have the best chance to win.

Flop: The first three community cards in Texas Hold'em and Omaha.

Gutshot: A straight draw that requires a card in the middle to hit to complete the straight. It is also called a "belly buster" and an "inside straight draw."

Hand: The cards in a player's hand or one game of poker in which a pot is won. When you hear or read this term, understand it in its context so you won't be confused.

Heads-Up: Playing against a single opponent.

Hole Cards: The first cards dealt to you that your opponents cannot see.

Implied Odds: Bets that you can reasonably expect to collect in addition to the bets already in the pot if you hit your hand.

Kicker: A card used to break ties. In Hold'em, if you have A-5 with an ace on the board, your 5 is your kicker. If an opponent also has an ace and their kicker is higher, you lose.

Limit: The set amount or amounts that may be bet, often expressed as 5/10 ($5 bets on the first two rounds and $10 bets thereafter).

Limp-In: To enter a hand with a call before the flop.

Loose: To play more hands than should be played.

Middle Pair: To have a pair containing the second highest card on the board.

Muck: To discard a hand.

Outs: Cards that can come that will improve your hand.

Overcard: A card that is higher than other cards, usually in reference to community cards that are higher than your hole cards.

Pair: Two cards that are the same rank (such as two kings).

Position: Your place in the order of betting action. If you act first, you are in first position.

Pot: All money that has been bet in a hand.

Pot Odds: The mathematical computation of the odds of your hand improving, the amount of money in the pot, and the size of the bet you must call.

Quads: Four of a kind (such as four aces).

Raise: To place a higher bet than an opponent has already placed.

Rake: The amount a card room takes from each pot, usually a percentage that has a set upper limit.

Reraise: To raise after an opponent has raised.

Seat Charge: The amount of money some card rooms charge per hour to play in addition to, or in place of, a rake.

Semibluff: To bet with a hand that may not be the best but has a good chance to improve to the best hand.

Set: Three of a kind (such as three jacks).

Short Stacked: To have the smallest stack of chips at the table.

Side Pot: An additional pot created when one player is all in and two or more other players are still betting.

Steal: To force an opponent to fold when you don't have the best hand.

Suited: Cards of the same suite (such as ♠4 and ♠7).

Tell: An action that a player makes that gives away the strength of their hand.

Tight: To play fewer hands than normal.

Tilt: When a player is emotionally upset and starts making poor decisions.

Trips: Three of a kind (such as three queens).

Under the Gun: The first person who must act on the first round of betting.

Wired Pair: When your hole cards contain a pair.